# Psychoanalytic Film Theory and *The Rules of the Game*

T0321541

# FILM THEORY IN PRACTICE

Series Editor: Todd McGowan

# Psychoanalytic Film Theory and *The Rules of the Game*

TODD MCGOWAN

Bloomsbury Academic
An imprint of Bloomsbury Publishing Inc

B L O O M S B U R Y
NEW YORK · LONDON · NEW DELHI · SYDNEY

**Bloomsbury Academic**

An imprint of Bloomsbury Publishing Inc

1385 Broadway
New York
NY 10018
USA

50 Bedford Square
London
WC1B 3DP
UK

**www.bloomsbury.com**

**BLOOMSBURY and the Diana logo are trademarks
of Bloomsbury Publishing Plc**

First published 2015

© Todd McGowan, 2015

**Library of Congress Cataloging-in-Publication Data**
A catalog record for this book is available from the Library of Congress

ISBN: HB: 978-1-6289-2084-0
PB: 978-1-6289-2082-6
ePub: 978-1-6289-2086-4
ePDF: 978-1-6289-2085-7

Series: Film Theory in Practice

Typeset by Deanta Global Publishing Services, Chennai, India

*For Quentin Martin*
*who taught me the rules of the game*
*while breaking them*

# CONTENTS

# ACKNOWLEDGMENTS

Thanks to Katie Gallof at Bloomsbury for pursuing this series of books and for trusting me with the weight of directing it. She has been a constant source of support and an enthusiastic partner.

My colleagues in film and television at the University of Vermont have been vitally important for my thinking about the cinema. Thanks to Deb Ellis, Dave Jenemann, Hilary Neroni, Sarah Nilsen, and Hyon Joo Yoo.

I am indebted theoretically to many fellow travelers, including Slavoj Žižek, Sheila Kunkle, Jennifer Friedlander, Henry Krips, Fabio Vighi, Rick Boothby, Frances Restuccia, Anna Kornbluh, Quentin Martin, Jean Wyatt, Ryan Engley, Jonathan Mulrooney, Louis-Paul Willis, Adam Cottrel, Hugh Manon, Danny Cho, Robyn Warhol, and Ken Reinhard.

Thanks especially to Walter Davis, Paul Eisenstein, and Hilary Neroni, who simply establish the rules for me.

# Introduction

## The intrinsic conjunction

It is surprising that psychoanalysis took as long as it did to gain a foothold in film theory. The connection between psychoanalytic thought and the cinema is readily apparent. It is not purely coincidental that both originated in the same year. In 1895, Freud and Joseph Breuer published *Studies on Hysteria*, and Louis and Auguste Lumière screened their first films in the Grand Café in Paris. Film theorists have often noted this historical connection, but it is not just the year of their origin that psychoanalysis and cinema have in common. Psychoanalysis makes its most important discoveries through the analysis of dreams, and to this day, the cinema remains a dream factory, a form of public dreaming.

Even though *Studies on Hysteria* marked the discovery of psychoanalysis as a talking cure for neurosis, the most important book in the development of psychoanalysis as a theory rather than just a therapeutic practice was *The Interpretation of Dreams*, which Freud alone published in 1900.[1] When he wrote a preface to the third English edition of the book, Freud reflected on his career to that point and claimed that this was his masterpiece. He said, "It contains, even according to my present-day judgment, the most valuable of all the discoveries it has been my good fortune to make. Insight such as this falls to one's lot but once in a lifetime."[2] Freud places such high regard on *The Interpretation of Dreams* because the book lays out the psychoanalytic theory of the structure of the psyche, and it does so through the analysis of dreams.

The basis of psychoanalysis is the discovery of the unconscious. The German Idealist Friedrich Schelling was the first to use the term "unconscious" (*unbewusst* in German) to describe the functioning of the mind, and several Romantic poets and philosophers, like Samuel Taylor Coleridge, picked up on this concept. But the unconscious of Romanticism is not the unconscious that Freud discovers. The Romantic unconscious is an inner self formed by emotions and feelings, and this unconscious doesn't appear externally. For Freud, the unconscious doesn't defy articulation but manifests itself through speech and other acts. In psychoanalysis, the unconscious is not a site of emotions and feelings. It instead houses a logic incompatible with the conscious mind, a logic oriented around desire. Freud takes an interest in dreams because they unlock the unconscious, and films, which share the structure of dreams, carry the same promise.

Of course, there is a fundamental difference between a dream and a film. An individual subject produces a dream, and a director, along with hundreds of others, creates a film. Even if the film provides insight into the psyche of the director, this has no inherent interest for anyone else. Thankfully, most likely due to the collective nature of film production, psychoanalytic film theory never wandered down the path of using the text as a window into the psyche of its creator in the way that literary criticism did during the middle of the twentieth century. No film theorist interpreted *La Règle du jeu* (*The Rules of the Game*, Jean Renoir 1939) as the product of Jean Renoir's hysteria in the way that psychoanalytic literary critics interpreted "The Purloined Letter" as the expression of Edgar Allan Poe's Oedipal desire. If film has value for what it reveals about the psyche, the psyche that it uncovers cannot simply be that of the director. Though the director's psyche undoubtedly plays a role in the form of the film, the fact that the film appeals to spectators indicates that it speaks to their psyches as well and to the structure of the psyche as such. Because it is a collective dream, the cinema reveals more precisely the psyche as such than any individual's dream does.

# The necessity of the disguise

Freud famously designates the dream as the fulfillment of a wish, though this fulfillment always occurs in a disguised form. I don't simply wish for a chocolate sundae and then dream about eating one. Freud absolutely rejects the possibility that dreams can directly represent what we desire. In fact, the necessity of disguise in a dream's act of fulfilling a wish leads Freud to the apparently bizarre conclusion that all dreams, apart from overtly sexual ones, have at their origin an erotic desire.[3] A dream never simply lays itself bare and gives the dreamer direct access to the desire that it satisfies. Prior to Freud, no one discovered the secret of dreams because of the role that disguise plays in their structure. One cannot just read dreams but must always interpret them.

Freud labels the process that disguises the subject's desire by translating it into the form of a dream "the dream work." The dream work involves constructing a series of images in the form of a more or less coherent narrative through which the dreamer finds her or his desire satisfied. It is unclear, however, why the disguise is necessary and why the dream work can't construct a dream that provides a direct satisfaction for the desire. The answer to this problem lies in Freud's theory of desire: desire is always illicit and always involves an unacceptable object.

Though we may have some desires for acceptable objects (like a good job, loving children, or a bowl of soup), desire as such is always illicit and aims at transgressing a social limit. We want the luxury suite in the hotel, a Rolls Royce, and a new romantic partner because they aren't readily available and because others don't have them. We associate enjoyment with these desires, and we enjoy the act of desiring. But even the desire to conform, to fit into a socially designated role, carries this excess of enjoyment with it. It is our inability not to enjoy our desire that renders it illicit. Every desire, from the most mundane to the most extravagant, touches on this excess that results in repression. The dream lifts repression and facilitates access to our desire, but it does so at the price of a distortion that occurs during the dream work.

In *The Interpretation of Dreams*, Freud contends that an agency he calls the censorship bears primary responsibility for the distortion that occurs in the wish fulfillment that dreams provide. Later, he would give the censorship a more precise name and call it the "superego."[4] The censorship or superego is an agency of prohibition that restricts the direct satisfaction of desire. We encounter everyday external agencies of prohibition that prevent us from realizing a wide variety of desires, like a traffic cop who forces us to slow down while driving on the highway or a boss who demands that we come to work on time. But psychoanalysis deduces the existence of an internal agency of prohibition that is much more exacting than these external ones. By prohibiting the direct realization of our desire, this internal agency enables the subject to obey external authorities more easily. Thanks to the internal prohibition, obeying the boss seems like second nature and not like continually bowing to a menacing authority figure.

Given the necessity of coexisting with others in society, the development of an internal agency of prohibition seems comprehensible. If subjects just did what they wanted and followed their desire with regard only to external restraint, life in common would become difficult. The society could not employ enough police officers to sustain order. The superego creates an internal police force that relieves the burden that actual police officers must face when subjects act on their desires.

But if the internal prohibition is just the integration of the external authority into the psyche that is done for the sake of smoothing out our external interactions, then it doesn't make sense that this prohibition affects and distorts dreams, which no one sees but the dreamer. There must be something traumatic about desire itself in order for the censorship or superego to concern itself with dreams rather than focusing solely on actions that involve others. The nature of the dream work—its distortion of a desire that has no effect at all on the external world—attests to the self-limiting nature of desire. Desire doesn't simply run into obstacles that prevent its realization but actually requires such obstacles to constitute it as desire. Desire depends on not realizing itself, and the dream work makes this clear.

The difference between everyday life and dreaming is that the former presents us with merely contingent obstacles to the realization of our desire while the latter shows that desire constructs necessary obstacles to its realization. Everyday life perpetuates the illusion that if only we had more money or were better looking we would attain what we desire. But the dream gives the lie to this illusion. When we dream, we encounter obstacles to the realization of our desire that our desire itself concocts. This is why Freud claims in *The Interpretation of Dreams* that "The interpretation of dreams is the royal road to a knowledge of the unconscious activities of the mind."[5] Dreams reveal the structure of our unconscious desire that everyday life obscures with a series of contingent obstacles to that desire.

## The necessity of the obstacle

Dreams present us with scenarios that show our desire encountering a necessary rather than a contingent obstacle. The absence of any interaction with the external world—no one else knows about our dreams unless we relate them to others—indicates that the distortion of our desire that takes place in dreams is a necessary distortion and lays bare the structure of our unconscious desire. The most conspicuous element of dreams as wish fulfillments is their failure to fulfill these wishes by simply providing the image of the object that we desire. This failure suggests that desire is much more complicated than it appears on the surface and reveals ultimately why desire must be unconscious.

When we examine our own desires through the activity of conscious reflection, we align these desires with objects of desire that would satisfy them. We desire a car, a candy bar, a gold necklace, a romantic partner, and so on. The relationship between the desire and its object seems straightforward. We want the object of desire, and we want to overcome the obstacle preventing us from having it. The object might cost too much money, have deleterious consequences on our health, belong to someone else, or not be amenable to our desire for whatever reason. But dreams, which are the fulfillment of wishes, do not depict the elimination of the obstacle and free access to the object of desire. Though dreams may end with dreamers having their objects, dreams also go to tremendous lengths to create obstacles barring the way to the realization of desire. These obstacles would be completely unnecessary if desire had a straightforward relationship to its object, but their existence tells us that it doesn't.

The effect of the dream work demands that we distinguish between the satisfaction of desire and desire's realization. Desire realizes itself when it obtains the object that it seeks, but desire satisfies itself through its failure to realize itself and obtain the object. In this sense, the obstacle that desire confronts is more important—and more satisfying—than the object of desire. The object of desire always disappoints the subject, but the obstacle to this object provides a constant source of satisfaction. We enjoy the barrier, which is why the most satisfying relationships are also the most troubling. The dream reveals that satisfaction and failure are inseparable.

One might say that every dream is a nightmare—or every film is a horror film—because it reveals to us the impossibility of our desire's realization. When we dream the fulfillment of a wish, we do so by dreaming the distortion of the wish in order to sustain the desire as a desire. Desire is traumatic because its satisfaction doesn't coincide with its realization (with obtaining the object), and the dream and the film make evident this disjunction through their investment in the obstacle as the source of satisfaction for the dreamer and the spectator. This type of revelation does not occur in everyday life, and we need the dream or the film in order to experience it.

Our everyday waking life resists the recognition of the disjunction between the satisfaction and the realization of desire. Consciousness plays a substantial role in everyday life, and its apparatus cannot accommodate the equation of satisfaction and failure. Consciousness views satisfaction in terms of success—scoring the winning goal, obtaining the new romantic partner, winning the lottery—but this image of success is antithetical to the way in which the unconscious satisfies itself. The unconscious is not simply what is not conscious but a completely different structure of relating to the world. There is a radical discontinuity between consciousness and the unconscious. We can think of the opposition between consciousness and the unconscious in terms of the contrast between will and desire.

The subject wills something actively through a conscious choice. One targets a goal through an act of will and then tries to achieve the goal. Unlike will, desire is always unconscious and irreducible to conscious manipulation. I cannot, for instance, simply decide to stop desiring ice cream, no matter how overweight I become or how unhealthy for my diabetic body my conscious mind knows it to be. In the case of ice cream, we can see how at odds will and desire are. Conscious will does not trump unconscious desire, and this failure of will in the face of desire is what gives birth to psychoanalysis.

The unconscious status of desire renders it difficult to know. One cannot gain access to one's desire by engaging in sustained and deep reflection on it. In this sense, psychoanalysis opposes itself to the history of philosophical introspection. The unconscious is not merely what escapes the awareness of conscious thoughts. It is instead what the subject cannot bring to consciousness, what is antithetical to conscious knowledge. But there are ways to access the unconscious: it appears when consciousness is not ready for it. We cannot know the unconscious, but we can encounter it when it takes us by surprise and jolts us into a new awareness.

In his psychoanalytic theory, Freud lays out four ways through which we can encounter the unconscious—dreams, jokes, slips, and free association. He devotes a book to each of the first three paths to the unconscious, and the last path provides the basis for psychoanalytic therapy.[6] But dreams have a privileged status among these paths. Only the distortion of the dream provides a definitive indication of the influence of the unconscious. Though most jokes and slips bear the mark of an unconscious influence, one can tell a joke that doesn't touch on the unconscious, and one can misspeak or forget an appointment without revealing one's unconscious desire. Likewise, free association can lead away from the unconscious rather than toward it. The dream, in contrast, always testifies to the activity of the unconscious, which is why Freud labels it, and not the joke or the slip, a "royal road."

A film is not a dream. But it is as close to a dream as we come in waking life. The key similarity is not what we might expect—that the medium replaces ideas with images, like the rebus and like the dream. While this is significant, the crucial parallel lies in the position of the subject in the dream and in the cinema. The cinema is just as much a royal road to the unconscious as the dream because it marginalizes conscious will and privileges unconscious desire more than any other artistic medium to this point in history.[7] When reading a novel, one must follow the plot of the novel, but the medium leaves one free to create one's own images of the events. The painting determines what one looks at, but it leaves the spectator's consciousness free to decide the duration and location of the look. Theater seems the closest art to cinema. It does focus the attention of the spectator on the stage and control the length of the performance. But the emphasis in theater is not on the images presented but on what characters say. It does not create a dreamlike world. The theater may activate the unconscious of spectators, but it must do so through their conscious interaction with the play. The cinema is uniquely positioned proximate to the dream, even though tangible differences remain.

# The form of desire

In contrast to dreams, films are conscious constructions and thus not the product of dream work, which would seem to limit the homology between dreams and films. If the dream work represents the key to dreams, its absence in the cinema would be significant. But there is a version of the dream work operative in the cinema, and it is the demands of film form. Just as psychoanalysis pays attention to the dream work in order to understand unconscious desire, psychoanalytic film theory focuses on film form in pursuit of the same end. The difference is that psychoanalysis concentrates on the desire of individual subjects while psychoanalytic film theory concerns itself with desire in a larger sense—either desire in a particular social situation or desire as such. The form of the film holds the secret not of the desire of the filmmaker but of the spectator.

The fact that someone else makes the film appears to function as a barrier to a psychoanalytic inquiry into the spectator made on the basis of the film. But on this level, the homology between the dream and the film holds complete. A filmmaker creates a film to satisfy the spectator's desire in the same way that a dreamer creates a dream in order to satisfy the subject's desire. Even though the filmmaker and the spectator are not the same person like the producer of the dream and the subject of it, in both cases the scenario exists for the sake of satisfying a desire.

Filmmakers make films not for their own pleasure but in order to appeal to the spectator's desire. Though one can think of films that aim to disturb spectators—like *Invasion of the Body Snatchers* (Philip Kaufman 1978) or *Kids* (Larry Clark 1995)—these films nonetheless target the desire of potential spectators, spectators who desire to be disturbed. There is no film, just as there is no dream, that doesn't engage in an appeal to the subject's desire.

Film theorists and critics often exhibit defensiveness about the popularity of film as an artistic medium. Its popularity seems at odds with its artistic pretensions. But for psychoanalytic film theory, the popularity of film testifies to its value as a medium for the interpretation of desire. In contrast to, say, sculpture, cinema has a wide appeal and arouses enough desire in spectators that they come in significant numbers to watch. The number of people who attended the opening of *Avatar* (James Cameron 2009) far outstrips the number who came out for the entire duration of the monumental joint exhibition of the sculptures of Auguste Rodin and Henry Moore in London from March 29 to October 27, 2013. This is not to say, of course, that film has more value than sculpture, just that it speaks to the contemporary subject's desire in a way that sculpture cannot. Film's popularity is the index of its appeal to our desire.

Often, however, the most important films are the ones that are the least popular. This is because our desire is never straightforward. We desire to be disturbed, and which is why films like *Invasion of the Body Snatchers* and *Kids* are popular—and also why the horror film has become a staple in contemporary cinema. But we also refuse our own desire or desire not to have our desire. In his discussion of the fulfillment of the wish in the dream, Jacques Lacan, the psychoanalyst responsible for making psychoanalysis more theoretical and even philosophical, points out that desire is always redoubled.[8] In his *Seminar VII: The Ethics of Psychoanalysis*, he says, "The dreamer … does not have a simple and unambiguous relationship to his wish. He rejects it, he censures it, he doesn't want it. Here we encounter the essential dimension of desire— it is always desire in the second degree, desire of desire."[9] Because desire is always desire of desire, we have the potential to flee from it and to neglect precisely those films that speak most profoundly to our desire. We do so because the encounter with our desire is always traumatic, and the great films don't disturb us in an appealing way like the garden-variety horror film but disturb us by facilitating a traumatic encounter with our unconscious desire.

The form of the film distorts the desire that it presents in a way homologous to the dream work. Though formal techniques in the cinema result from a conscious agency producing them and the unconscious that structures the dream work, they both serve the same function—the distortion of desire into a series of images in some semblance of a narrative structure. Even films that appear to disdain narrative structure altogether, like Germaine Dulac's *La coquille et le clergyman* (*The Seashell and the Clergyman*, 1928) or Luis Buñuel's *Un chien andalou* (1929), inevitably fall into it through their juxtaposition of images. In fact, after two or three viewings, the narrative of these famous surrealist films becomes clear. Similarly, narrative plays a decisive role in even the most oddly constructed dream. The narrative functions as a fantasy scenario through which subjects can satisfy their desire.

The various formal decisions that occur during the making of a film to constitute the narrative reveal the spectator's desire. Unlike the dream, cinema is not a direct expression of the subject's desire but an attempt to lure or arouse this desire. A director uses montage during one scene, deep focus in another, and a series of close-ups for a third. These choices affect how the spectator's desire relates to what transpires on the screen. The psychoanalytic film theorist approaches a film like the psychoanalyst approaches a dream. One interprets the formal structure to show how the film speaks to the desire of the spectator and what the film reveals about this desire.

But the formal techniques of the cinema do not have one significance that remains the same for every film. That is to say, the use of deep focus doesn't always signify that the desires of the characters in the foreground match those in the background (though it certainly might signify this). Each formal technique exists in relation to the overall structure of the film, and the theorist must interpret it in this sense. A film could use deep focus to show the psychic distance separating characters rather than their similarity.[10] Interpretation is not mere substitution— the replacement of a formal technique with a psychic structure. Instead, psychoanalytic interpretation involves examining the form of the film as it relates to the unconscious. Every film, even the most banal, speaks to the unconscious in some way and necessitates psychoanalytic interpretation. But this form of interpretation is exigent when films disturb spectators despite not having a disturbing content. We expect films about the Holocaust like *Nuit et brouillard* (*Night and Fog*, Alain Resnais 1955) or other horrific subjects to be disturbing, but we don't expect it with *The Rules of the Game*, a narrative about a holiday in the country for the wealthy.[11]

## Psychoanalysis and *The Rules of the Game*

Some films are not popular when they appear, simply because they fail to speak to the spectator's desire at all. This is often the case with famous bombs in the history of cinema like Elaine May's *Ishtar* (1987) or Kevin Reynolds' *Waterworld* (1995). But this is not true of *The Rules of the Game*. Renoir made the film at the height of his popularity. His great film from two years earlier, *La Grande Illusion* (*The Grand Illusion*, 1937), was the first foreign-language film ever nominated for an Academy Award, and it garnered prizes at film competitions around the world. While not as popular as *La Grande Illusion*, Renoir's subsequent film, *La Bête humaine* (*The Human Beast*, 1938), was also a success. *The Rules of the Game*, however, outraged audiences, and critics assailed it for its confusing structure. The fact that it is now almost universally considered among the ten greatest films ever made does not obviate its original reception. The contemporary appreciation for the film highlights the disturbance that it initially caused.

*The Rules of the Game* is an odd choice for a psychoanalytic interpretation. Unlike a film like Alfred Hitchcock's *Vertigo* (1958), which is clearly about a desiring subject and his construction of a fantasy to realize that desire, Renoir's film has characters that seem bereft of any psychic complexity. They simply play out their assigned social roles unthinkingly. There is no compelling character that the spectator must strive to comprehend. Instead, the motives of everyone are apparent and on the surface. But a lack of psychic complexity is not the same as a lack of insight into the psyche. In fact, the banality of the characters that Renoir creates speaks to their significance for understanding the psyche of the subject as such. He does not paint the exception but the rule (as the title suggests). This accounts both for the initial disturbance that the film caused and for its lasting resonance among spectators.

No one appreciates being confronted with her or his own conformity. Even those who conform want to believe that they are acting independently. But *The Rules of the Game* gives the lie to this pretension of independence and reveals how widespread obedience is in modern society, despite the fact that modernity proclaims autonomy as its cardinal virtue. As the film shows, obedience lingers even at the moments when we believe ourselves to be most independent because authority appeals to subjects through their desire. Subjects have an unconscious investment in the power of social authority that leads to a surplus obedience, an obedience that goes further than the authority itself requires. *The Rules of Game* disturbs spectators by revealing to them the extent of their fealty to the authority that they believe themselves to have escaped.

# Notes

1   *The Interpretation of Dreams* actually appeared late in 1899, but Freud convinced the publisher to date the book in the new century in order to indicate the epochal nature of his discoveries. As a result, 1900 has become the accepted date of publication for the book.

2   Sigmund Freud, Preface to the Third English Edition, *The Interpretation of Dreams* (I), trans. James Strachey, in *The Standard Edition of the Complete Psychological Works of Sigmund Freud*, vol. 4, ed. James Strachey (London: Hogarth, 1953), xxxii.

3 Freud makes this point very clearly in his short version of *The Interpretation of Dreams* that he wrote for a more popular audience entitled *On Dreams*. There, Freud claims, "most of the dreams of adults are traced back by analysis to *erotic wishes*. This assertion is not aimed at dreams with an *undisguised* sexual content, which are no doubt familiar to all dreamers from their own experience and are as a rule the only ones to be described as 'sexual dreams'" (Sigmund Freud, *On Dreams*, trans. James Strachey, in *The Standard Edition of the Complete Psychological Works of Sigmund Freud*, vol. 5, ed. James Strachey [London: Hogarth, 1953], 682). Overtly sexual dreams do not originate from erotic desires, a fact that Freud deduces from the necessity of distortion in the dream work.

4 When he wrote *The Interpretation of Dreams* in 1899, Freud adhered to the topographical model of the psyche that divided it into conscious, preconscious, and unconscious. Much later, Freud developed a new model for understanding the psyche known as the structural model. The structural model, first articulated in 1923 in *The Ego and the Id*, theorizes the psyche in terms of id, ego, and superego. The superego is the agency of authority and law within the psyche, and thus it comes to play the part that the censorship did in the earlier theory.

5 Sigmund Freud, *The Interpretation of Dreams* (II), in *The Standard Edition of the Complete Psychological Works of Sigmund Freud*, vol. 5, trans. and ed. James Strachey (London: Hogarth, 1953), 608.

6 For Freud's discussion of slips, see Sigmund Freud, *The Psychopathology of Everyday Life*, trans. James Strachey, in *The Standard Edition of the Complete Psychological Works of Sigmund Freud*, vol. 6, ed. James Strachey (London: Hogarth, 1960). For Freud's analysis of jokes, see Sigmund Freud, *Jokes and Their Relation to the Unconscious*, trans. James Strachey, in *The Standard Edition of the Complete Psychological Works of Sigmund Freud*, vol. 8, ed. James Strachey (London: Hogarth, 1960).

7 It is possible that someone will invent a new medium that will marginalize consciousness even more than cinema, and some filmmakers have imagined this possibility. In the remarkable *Until the End of the World* (Wim Wenders 1991), Wenders

imagines a machine that enables people to immerse their conscious minds within their dreams, and in *Strange Days* (Kathryn Bigelow 1995), Bigelow posits the invention of a device that allows people to experience what others experienced by connecting the device to other people's brains. But most new developments in visual media—especially the rise of interactivity—represent a turn away from the unconscious and a move toward increasing the subject's conscious control.

8   Though commentators often credit Lacan with bringing semiotics or structural linguistics into psychoanalytic thought, his fundamental contribution is grasping the philosophical implications of Freud's discoveries. His training during the 1930s with the most important Hegelian philosopher of the twentieth century, Alexandre Kojève, laid the groundwork for this contribution.

9   Jacques Lacan, *The Seminar of Jacques Lacan*, *Book VII: The Ethics of Psychoanalysis, 1959-1960*, ed. Jacques-Alain Miller, trans. Dennis Porter (New York: Norton, 1992), 14.

10   The use of deep focus to emphasize distance actually occurs in the most famous deep focus shot in film history—the moment when the young Charles Foster Kane (Buddy Swan) plays outside in the snow while his mother Mary (Agnes Moorehead) signs the agreement to place him in the custody of Mr Thatcher (George Coulouris) in Orson Welles' *Citizen Kane* (1941).

11   If a film about the Holocaust is not disturbing enough, this is itself disturbing. The problem with Steven Spielberg's *Schindler's List* (1993) is that Spielberg managed what seems unthinkable: he created an uplifting Holocaust film.

# CHAPTER ONE

# Psychoanalytic film theory

## The unconscious

The foundation of psychoanalysis is the unconscious. Psychoanalysis emerges with the discovery of the disturbance that unconscious thoughts cause in the daily life of neurotic subjects and how it shapes the dreams of even nonneurotic subjects. But this is instantly a problem because the existence of the unconscious portends the absence of any possible foundation for knowledge. Despite Freud's hope that psychoanalysis would attain the status of a science, the impossibility of realizing this hope lies within the heart of the psychoanalytic project itself. Psychoanalysis reveals that knowledge is never simply knowledge but that desire always accompanies it, that desire always trumps knowledge when it comes to how we act. The unconscious is this desire from which knowledge can never extricate itself.[1]

The cinema attracts spectators because it ignites their desire, and psychoanalysis is a philosophy of desire. Psychoanalytic theory provides insight into the most basic question that confronts the study of film: Why does someone go to see and enjoy a film? To address this question, I will explain the key concepts from psychoanalysis that lead to a possible response.

These concepts are desire, fantasy, enjoyment, demand, the real, the symbolic order, the imaginary, and the lost object. The discussion will focus on Freud and Jacques Lacan to the exclusion of all other psychoanalytic thinkers because Freud and Lacan have had the most influence on film theory and because their specific concepts speak more cogently to the cinematic situation than those of other thinkers. The point of psychoanalysis is to bring the subject to the point where it can recognize itself in its seemingly alien unconscious desire, and through this recognition, the subject gains a freedom to act, a freedom that doesn't ignore the unconscious but embraces it. Understood through psychoanalytic theory, cinema can become integral to this same process of freedom. But one must approach it with the unconscious as the point of departure.

The unconscious is not simply what is not conscious. If it were, then it would not cause the disturbance to psychic equilibrium that it causes. The unconscious is rather radically distinct from consciousness and functions in a completely different way. In his early thought, Freud distinguishes between three registers—consciousness, the preconscious, and the unconscious.[2] According to Freud, consciousness includes only what one has in one's mind at the moment, which gives it a very limited purview. The preconscious is much more expansive and encompasses all of the knowledge that one can bring to consciousness without any effort. For instance, the fact that Thomas Jefferson was the third president of the United States exists in my preconscious. If someone asks me who the third president was, I can respond without undergoing psychoanalysis to bring the answer to the fore of my thinking. With the unconscious, however, the situation is altogether different.

Freud separates the unconscious from consciousness and the preconscious because we cannot simply make unconscious material conscious by concentrating on it. The unconscious never comes to consciousness without some form of traumatic disruption. The trauma associated with the unconscious stems from the role that desire plays in its structure. While the subject's interests can be conscious, its desire cannot be. One can consciously pursue one's self-interest with ease, but desire does not fit so neatly into consciousness. The problem is that the subject's desire is opposed to and undermines the subject's self-interest. Desire has a traumatic charge because the subject desires against its own good, and this is one of the fundamental discoveries of psychoanalysis, a discovery that places psychoanalysis in opposition to almost the entire history of philosophy and to common sense, which sees our good (or happiness) as the unquestioned aim of all our actions.

The unconscious doesn't just exist apart from consciousness but acts as an existential threat to consciousness. It is as if an alien were residing within the psyche of the subject, which is why the subject has no direct access to it and must resort to dreams, slips, jokes, works of art, or the psychoanalytic session in order to access it. When psychoanalytic theorists after Freud minimize the alien status of the unconscious and its difference from consciousness, they mute the power of the psychoanalytic project. This happened most obviously in the United States with the development of ego psychology. Heinz Hartmann's classic work *Ego Psychology and the Problem of Adaptation* is the emblem of the retreat from the unconscious, but the instances are widespread throughout the psychoanalytic world.[3] In fact, it is the failure of other psychoanalysts to sustain the radicality of the unconscious that prompts Jacques Lacan to argue for the necessity of a "return to Freud" in the 1950s. But the threat of a turn away from the unconscious remains a constant danger in psychoanalytic theory even in the wake of Lacan.

This danger manifests itself when one replaces the term "unconscious" with "subconscious," as often happens today. No one who has any allegiance at all to the psychoanalytic project would perform such a misleading exchange of terms. French psychologist Pierre Janet coined the word "subconscient," which became "subconscious" in English. The problem with this concept is that it minimizes the alien status of the unconscious and serves to domesticate it. Freud specifically inveighs against the use of the term for exactly this reason.[4] Freud's unconscious is distinct both from the subconscious and from earlier versions of the unconscious that appeared in the century before psychoanalysis emerged.

Historians often credit German Romantic poets and philosophers with inventing the idea that part of the mind is *unbewusst* or unconscious. It is the case that this word certainly predates Freud. But for the Romantics, the unconscious is situated deep within the psyche. It is the seat of emotions and feelings that I am not aware that I have but that no one else has any awareness of either. This is the decisive point of difference. For Freud, I don't know my unconscious, but others do when they hear my slips of the tongue, see my tics, and listen to my jokes. The Romantic philosopher uses reflection and internal probing to access this unconscious, but Freud sees the unconscious as wholly inaccessible by such methods. One can safely say that Freud discovered the unconscious because, though others use the term prior to him, he was the first to situate the unconscious not in the depths but on the surface of the psyche, manifesting itself in how the subject speaks and acts. The unconscious is an alien within, but this alien constantly intrudes on the subject's everyday life by distorting how the subject perceives and knows the world. The unconscious is hidden, but it is hidden in plain sight. The unconscious affects every aspect of conscious life despite its radical difference from consciousness.

The unconscious is not housed deep within the psyche, which is why one cannot simply replace psychoanalysis with introspection.[5] We reveal ourselves through what we say and how we act, not through what we think about what we say and how we act, which is why no amount of thinking about why we acted as we did will unlock the unconscious. The key to it lies outside ourselves. The psychoanalyst draws our attention away from our reflection on our words and actions by focusing on the words and actions themselves. The unconscious expresses itself in words and actions rather than lurking behind them in our thoughts, where we tend to locate it.

If we understand that the unconscious expresses itself in the subject's comportment, the importance of film for psychoanalysis becomes clear. Films translate unconscious desire into a series of images that we can analyze. Subjects could not say what the film is able to reveal about them when it arouses their unconscious desire, precisely because this desire is unconscious. Though no subject desires exactly like another, cinema provides a site for the formulation of desires that are widespread and rooted within the social order. In the filmic experience, the unconscious shows itself on the screen.

As Freud conceives it, the unconscious possesses an extimate status—at once inside and outside. It is a surface phenomenon that doesn't belong to an individual subject in the way that the Romantics envisioned but emerges through the subject's relationship to the social order. This relationship is one of mutual interdependence in which the social order requires the participation of the subject and the subject desires through the social order. To say that the subject has an unconscious—or, more precisely, that the unconscious has the subject—is to say that the subject is always a desiring subject.

If one refuses to grant the primacy of unconscious desire for the subject, one leaves the terrain of psychoanalysis altogether. This is Freud's revolutionary insight, and he abandons those who abandon this insight, as the case of Alfred Adler reveals. Adler was one of Freud's early followers and a member of the Vienna Psychoanalytic Society that Freud headed. Adler was a respected associate, but Freud's refusal to give ground on the status of the subject as a desiring being precipitates his break with Adler. Though historians of psychoanalysis often characterize Freud as intolerant of dissent and blame his break with Adler on this intolerance, there is a clear theoretical cause for the break, even though it may also be true that he was, like any committed theorist, intolerant of dissent. By transforming sexual desire into the pursuit of power (and the flight from the feeling of inferiority), Adler strips away the essential kernel of Freud's discovery. In 1908, Freud exiled Adler from the Vienna Psychoanalytic Society due to this heterodox concept of desire, despite his admiration for Adler as a thinker. The slippage from the subject of desire to the subject of power is slight, but in the distance separating them the entire radicality of Freud's discovery resides.[6]

Adler's thesis that the quest for power and the avoidance of powerlessness motivate the subject has the effect of eliminating the unconscious. According to psychoanalysis, desire is unconscious because the subject cannot translate it into a conscious project. One cannot say what it is that the subject desires, and it is this irreducibility of desire to consciousness that gives birth to psychoanalysis. But once Adler replaces desire with power, its irreducibility to consciousness disappears. If we want power, it is quite easy to name the object of our desire. On this basis, one can imagine (as Adler does) the possibility for political improvements in which society distributes power more evenly and thus facilitates the satisfaction of more desire.

On the surface, Adler seems clearly like a more politically astute figure than Freud. In fact, he turns to the idea of power in order to account for the impact of political arrangements—like patriarchal society—on the subject. What's more, his overt political commitments and activities certainly outstrip those of Freud. But to conclude that Adler's turn from desire to power is a more politically efficacious version of psychoanalytic theory would be to move much too hastily. By eliminating the priority of desire and de facto relegating the unconscious to inexistence, Adler creates a system in which the subject no longer fails to fit in to the ruling social order. As a result, his system, despite his attempt to politicize psychoanalysis, portends the end of politics, since political contestation depends on the fact that the individual's desire cannot be reconciled with the social order. If we imagine that power motivates us, then we simultaneously imagine ourselves as beings that wholly belong to the social order that produces us.

Adler's assault on Freud's foundational idea of the subject with an unconscious desire remains alive today, though it doesn't appear under the banner of Adler. Adler's turn from desire to power presages the critique of Freud that Michel Foucault authors in his *History of Sexuality*, *Volume 1* and that Judith Butler takes up in her *Gender Trouble*. Though we associate both theorists with politics, Foucault and Butler have difficulty theorizing political change because they reject desire for the sake of power and thereby lose the disjunction between the subject and the social order. These two figures have a dominant presence in the contemporary theoretical landscape, and their dominance threatens to silence the psychoanalytic conception of desire at a time when the theoretical need for this conception is pressing. Biology now threatens to explain everything, and desire remains a rampart against it.[7]

# Biology and culture

Psychoanalytic theory insists on the difference between the desiring subject and the biological entity that becomes the desiring subject. In the contemporary world, we are constantly pulled between two competing explanations of our actions. The scientist wants to explain actions in terms of evolutionary patterns of behavior, the structure of our DNA, or the way that our brains function. According to this position, human evolution requires polygamous males, and I find myself inevitably drawn to have an affair despite my satisfying long-term relationship. The cultural critic, in contrast, seeks an explanation for these same actions in the exigencies of society. I have an affair not for evolutionary reasons but because I live in a patriarchal culture that identifies male sexual conquests with phallic authority. Psychoanalysis doesn't pick a side in this battle but opts instead to reject both explanations. In doing so, it insists that I take responsibility for my affair, which it locates in my desire rather than in my nature or in my culture.

The response that psychoanalytic theory gives to the alternatives of nature and culture is akin to Immanuel Kant's response to what he calls the mathematical antinomies of pure reason. These antinomies involve the opposed claims that the world either does have a beginning in space and time or doesn't and that there is a simple substance in the world or there isn't. Kant solves these antinomies not by opting for one position or the other—by claiming that the world has a beginning in space and time, for instance—but by claiming that both alternatives are wrong. Instead of taking a side in response to the question, he insists that the object of the question doesn't exist. The world doesn't have a beginning but neither has it existed forever. Kant resolves the dilemma by claiming that there is no such thing as the world in the sense of a whole that might either begin or not begin.[8]

Psychoanalysis makes precisely the same point with regard to the ever-popular—and ever-tedious—question of nature or culture. According to psychoanalytic theory, the answer is not a little of both but neither. Though theorists take strong positions on one side or the other, common sense today forges a compromise—seeing a blend of nature and culture determining us. But this position represents a failure to recognize how nature and culture interact. Just as Kant rejects the existence of a whole world that would begin or not begin, psychoanalytic theory insists that neither the pure human animal nor the pure product of culture exists. Though there have been feral children, they are like other animals until they encounter a social order, at which point they cease to be simply human animals and become subjects of desire. In the same way, there is no cultural being that enters fully into the culture. Such a being would be the equivalent of a Stepford wife, perfectly adapted to a societal role without any remainder.

The subject is not a synthesis of the biological entity and the culture it enters but a product of the violent collision of the one with the other. This is not simply a presupposition or axiom of psychoanalytic theory that one must accept or reject but a conclusion revealed by the way that the subject comports itself relative to its animality and to its culture. The subject does not act like an animal nor does it act like a being of culture. Neither position fits the subject. When the human animal enters into language, it undergoes a radical transformation. It doesn't retain its prior animality, nor does it become a fully cultural being. Instead, it can exist in neither location and becomes necessarily alienated from both. The signifier deprives the animal of its instincts and replaces those instincts with desires, which are the product of its subjection.

This has important implications for considering the cinema. From this psychoanalytic perspective, we don't watch films because they satisfy a need or because society commands that we do so. Both of these positions are obviously false. There must be another driving force compelling us to watch, and this is where psychoanalytic theory intervenes. It privileges desire, which is neither biological nor cultural, as the unconscious motivation for our acts, and this is never more apparent than it is with the cinema.

Two of the most seductive paths for abandoning psycho-analysis are biologism and culturalism. The former treats the subject as an animal and reduces its desire to animal instinct, while the latter treats the subject as a cultural construction and reduces desire to the societal good. In the history of psychoanalysis, culturalism has served as the predominant heresy. The main figures of this position are Karen Horney and Erich Fromm. Increasingly, however, culturalists oppose themselves to psychoanalytic theory altogether, and biologism is making inroads as some evolutionary biologists claim that Freud anticipated their scientific findings. But the problem with both biologism and culturalism is that they fail to account for the distortion that occurs when the individual is subjected to language. This traumatic event provides the point of departure for Jacques Lacan's intervention in psychoanalytic theory.

# Need, demand, and desire

Lacan's importance as a psychoanalytic theorist stems from his grasp of the disruption that occurs with the subjection of human animals to the signifier. This subjection has such a distorting effect that we cannot use the terms "human being" or "person" to describe the speaking being but must instead employ the term "subject." Lacan analyzes the subjection of human animal to the signifier with three terms that account for the three positions involved—the animal prior to its subjection, the moment that subjection occurs, and its result. Initially, the human animal is a being of need, but when this being of need encounters the demand that accompanies the introduction of the signifying order, desire emerges. These three concepts enable us to understand the foundations of psychoanalytic theory and how we can think about its relationship to the cinema.

The human animal has instincts or needs that must be met in order for it to satisfy itself. If the human animal never encountered language, it would continue to satisfy these needs like other animals. It would find satisfaction by eating when hungry and by having sex when moved by the instinct to reproduce. Need operates in a straightforward fashion, but the signifier disrupts this straightforwardness.

In the social order, the individual must meet these needs through the mediation of a demand that accompanies the signifier. Demand, as Lacan theorizes it, has two distinct but related senses: it is the subject's demand for love or recognition and the social order's demand for the subject's obedience. In both cases, the signifier is the vehicle for the demand: the subject demands recognition through what it says, and the social order demands obedience through what it tells the subject. By forcing needs into the caldron of demand, the social order completely transforms these needs. The subject can no longer simply eat to satisfy its hunger or have sex to satisfy its sexual urge. Instead, it has to satisfy its needs through the mediation of the social demand, so that a desire emerges in response to this intersection. The subject does not just transfer its need to demand because it cannot locate satisfaction directly in the demand.

Demand alone does not dictate how the subject satisfies itself due to the distorting influence of the signifier. Demand arrives through a signifier—the social authority says, "Do this, don't do that," in language, and the subject articulates its demand for love with words—but the signifier is not transparent. Whenever we hear a demand, the opaqueness of the signifier leads us to suppose that a desire resides behind the demand. When I hear someone ask me something, I always wonder what she or he really wants from me. When a parent tells a child to obey at all times, the parent doesn't desire total obedience but rather obedience with an occasional infraction. No authority figure desires subjects who follow their demands to the letter. Inversely, the subject desires more from authority figures than it demands. A child demands a snack after school but really wants proof of love, which the snack fails to provide. This is how desire subtends every demand. The demand is spoken, but the desire can't be. It is impossible for the subject simply to take a demand at face value, and yet the demand alienates the subject from its own needs. As a result, we are fundamentally subjects of desire, and this represents the point of departure for psychoanalytic theory.

In "The Signification of the Phallus," Lacan provides what has become a canonical explanation of the relationship between need, demand, and desire. He says, "Desire is neither the appetite for satisfaction nor the demand for love, but the difference that results from the subtraction of the first from the second, the very phenomenon of their splitting (*Spaltung*)."[9] That is to say, the subject's desire results from an initial demand for love that is unsatisfied. The subject demands love and receives baby formula or a diaper change instead. But the subject desires what exceeds the satisfaction of its need, and this excess is what the demand never receives. In this sense, desire exists because demand cannot be satisfied in the same way that needs can.

The influence of demand and the signifier on need is such that the desire that emerges is what the subject interprets the Other—the figure or figures of social authority, the one or ones whom the subject supposes to have authority—to desire. The subject does not begin with its own unique and singular desire that is subsequently alienated in the Other as a result of conformity to the Other's desire. I don't first desire to watch horror films and then begin to desire romantic comedies when I see that everyone else desires them. On the contrary, even my initial desire to watch horror films reflects the influence of what I imagine the Other desires. If I didn't suppose that the Other desired to watch horror films, I would never desire to watch them in the first place. In fact, their existence as possible objects of desire informs me that the Other does desire them, at least to some extent. The Other's desire provides me a way to orient my desire.

The encounter with the signifier gives the Other priority in relation to the desiring subject. I begin to desire only after I encounter the Other via the signifier. The desire of the Other comes first, but the subject knows this desire only through interpretation. One of Lacan's most well-known and repeated dictums is that our "desire is the desire of the Other," which means that our desire is not originally our own but an interpretation of the Other's desire (as manifested in a demand).[10] This works in two discrete but related ways.

We desire the Other to desire us. We act in order to arouse the desire of the Other for us. But even more importantly, we also pattern our own desire on what the Other desires. For instance, if the Other seems to desire a certain type of car, this desire becomes our desire as well. If the Other seems to desire a certain song, we will teach ourselves to desire and appreciate that song. Popular music reveals the power of the desire of the Other as well as any other realm. Few like a new song the first time they hear it, but we begin to like it after hearing it multiple times on the radio because this informs us about the Other's desire. Or we desire the popular people at school because we see that others desire them. This conformity of desire is not a weakness on our part but stems from the structure of desire.

But because desire is the desire of the Other, it doesn't achieve satisfaction through realizing itself as instinct does. An animal feels the instinct of hunger, and then it eats and finds satisfaction. We feel a desire for a piece of chocolate cake, but even as we're eating it, we think of what we might like to have later that would be better than the chocolate cake. Or while we're having sex with one person, we think about another. Even if we manage to have our perfect object, we will still experience dissatisfaction with the act of obtaining it. This is because we are desiring rather than instinctual beings.

For psychoanalysis, desire emerges through the encounter with the Other's demand and the interpretation of the Other's desire that results from this encounter. Desire doesn't exist prior to the demand except in the form of animal need. Thus, even though the demand asks for our obedience, it does have the effect of freeing us from the unthinking necessity of our natural needs. Desire is at once alienating and freeing, and it is freeing to the extent that it is alienating. Prior to the onset of desire, the human animal can satisfy itself only through obtaining objects of satisfaction, but desire provides a wholly different path to satisfaction. The desiring subject satisfies itself through its desire rather than through the realization of that desire. The psychoanalytic view of satisfaction appears counterintuitive insofar as it emphasizes a type of satisfaction that doesn't involve obtaining the object that we desire.

This strange form of satisfaction through not obtaining the object is the result of the distortion that the human animal undergoes through its encounter with language. Though Freud chronicles the effects of this distortion through his discovery of the unconscious, it is Lacan who gives the encounter with language a privileged place in psychoanalytic theory. Lacan conceives of the symbolic order as the force that distorts the existence of the animal subjected to it and that produces the unconscious as the manifestation of this distortion.

## The symbolic order

Lacan uses three categories to classify the experience of the subject. These categories are the symbolic, imaginary, and real. The symbolic order is the order of language, and it provides the background of signification for the subject's actions. But Lacan insists that this order is always incomplete, which is why the imaginary and real must supplement it. In a certain sense, the imaginary and real are opposed. The imaginary register creates a sense of wholeness for the subject, and the real is the absence or incompletion that undermines every symbolic order. With its illusion of wholeness, the imaginary enables the subject to evade the confrontation with the real.

Lacan is often thought of as the thinker who brought an emphasis on language to psychoanalysis. He reinterprets the insights of Freud in light of structural linguistics, specifically the thought of Ferdinand de Saussure, Roman Jakobson, and Emile Benveniste. The signifier becomes the key to the structure of the social order. Society is structured by language, which forms the basis of the symbolic order. Saussure insists on the divide between the signifier and the signified, a divide that separates signification from meaning.[11] But Saussure also believes that signification arises not through a direct relationship between the signifier and the signified but out of the differences between signifiers and the differences between signifieds. That is to say, I know what a table is through differentiating it from a chair and a bed, not through identifying the word "table" with an actual table. This represents a landmark breakthrough, but Lacan would take this revolution in linguistics one step further.

When he considers the relationship between the signifier and the signified, Saussure grants the signified priority: meaning is more important than the word that designates the meaning. Lacan reverses this valuation and theorizes that the signifier has priority in relationship to the signified: how one says something becomes more important than—or determines—what one means. This turn toward the priority of the signifier is an important step in the development of Lacan's thought, and he is basically following the fundamental rule of psychoanalysis when he comes up with this idea.

In the psychoanalytic session, Freud establishes one rule: one must say whatever comes to mind without censoring oneself, and the analyst pays more attention to what one says than what one means. To take the most obvious example, if after I say "mother," I stop and say that I meant "girlfriend," the analyst will attach more importance to what I said than to what I say that I meant. What I say always outstrips what I mean. The signifier is the vehicle for my unconscious desire, and what I mean to say represents a way of trying to avoid a confrontation with that desire.[12] The significance of what we say isn't held inside us but exists outside in the signifiers. In other words, we don't speak language; language speaks us. The idea that we communicate a meaning that we have in mind before we speak is a lure that has its basis in a failure to grasp the priority of signifier for the subject.

The priority of the signifier has dramatic ramifications for the analysis of film. Once one understands that what one says or the film that one makes signifies beyond what one means, the filmmaker loses all authority over her or his creation. The critic or spectator has just as much of an opportunity to weigh in on the significance of a film as the filmmaker. The meaning that the filmmaker tries to communicate—if such a meaning did exist—becomes insignificant in the face of the symbolic text that the filmmaker creates. The significance of this text lies not in the filmmaker's (imaginary) meaning but in the text itself where anyone can interpret it. The structure of the symbolic order strips the author (or auteur) of her or his authority.

But the symbolic order is not just language. The symbolic is the structure that informs and gives a form to the reality that we experience. The symbolic is the specific structure of signifiers that creates meaning in the world and that gives us a sense of identity. Our symbolic identity includes our name and our professional status, and it is always attached to a structure that derives from the society. Without the symbolic order, nothing would have any significance at all. It provides a common background for us to interact with each other. It is the third party necessary for every exchange. We inhabit a shared symbolic order with others, but what Lacan calls the big Other (or an anonymous social authority) controls that symbolic order. We are in the grip of the big Other whenever we follow the reign of common sense, which tells us what to do without telling us anything. Common sense, as a tool of the big Other, works by not seeming to do anything at all. But this big Other doesn't exist on its own; it has power over us only insofar as we collectively invest ourselves in it, and this investment is what occurs when we accede to ideological interpellation.

The symbolic order is based on language, but it also includes the system of codes—both articulated and nonarticulated—that regulate our quotidian existence. The symbolic order provides the written laws that govern our actions, but the big Other is the source of the unspoken rules that support our social existence. Life together would be impossible without these rules, and for psychoanalysis, they play a much more important role than the written laws of a society. The unwritten rules provide a complex background that informs all our social interactions: they indicate how we should greet each other, what degree of informality to use in different encounters, even what we should do with our free time. Without the unwritten rules given to us by the big Other, we would have no guide for how to live our lives.

One of the great virtues of cinema is its ability to make explicit these unwritten rules that provide the glue that holds the social order together. This is what makes film noir a significant development in the history of cinema. The typical film noir depicts characters who violate society's written laws—Walter Neff (Fred MacMurray) commits murder in *Double Indemnity* (Billy Wilder 1944), for instance—but they nonetheless adhere to the most fundamental unwritten rule of society for American males: do whatever one can to make money and have sex with attractive women. Though noir shows the characters who follow the unwritten rule coming to ruin, it also highlights the power of this rule in determining the characters' actions. The unwritten rule is so powerful that the noir hero experiences his life as if it were directed by fate. As the example of film noir suggests, film offers us a space for the exploration of the unwritten rules that the symbolic order lays down and that remain invisible in everyday life.

But the unwritten rules are not simply guidelines for our actions. They often demand that we violate written laws. For instance, they tell us to drive a little bit faster than the speed limit, to eat a few grapes at the grocery store without paying for them, or to help a friend cover up her or his infidelities. The symbolic order binds us together as subjects, and the unwritten rules play a major part in this social bond. One can violate the written laws of a society and still belong to it (even if one belongs in prison), but the violation of the unwritten rules often leads to social exile. If one refuses to adhere to the unwritten rules governing bathing or appearance, social exile is not only likely but almost assured. But if one cheats on one's taxes, no such exile is forthcoming, even in the unlikely event of being caught. The unwritten rules have this importance because they provide the unifying force of the social order.

The symbolic order unites subjects not through what it officially proclaims but through unwritten rules that provide a secret code for those who belong and always trip up those who don't. The unwritten rules are more important than written laws in forming social cohesion because of their exclusivity. Anyone can access and learn the written laws, but only those with inside knowledge and years of experience can master the unwritten rules. In this way, they function ideologically to keep certain subjects out—like immigrants, other ethnics groups, other religious groups, and so on. The symbolic order excludes these outsiders in order to give the insiders a sense of belonging. Some must be cast out in order that some might be saved. The signifier creates identity through difference, and difference requires exclusion.

The symbolic order never includes everyone or everything. We never arrive at the last word that would make the symbolic order complete, which is why the symbolic order relies on exclusion to provide the pretense of a wholeness that it can never attain. It creates a division between those who belong and those who don't, and it uses the unwritten rules to do so. Though the symbolic order seems to promise universal inclusion, this is always illusory. The belonging of some depends on the exclusion of others, and the symbolic order acts as a border guard enforcing this distinction between those inside and those outside.

## The real

Even though the symbolic order provides the background for all interactions, it cannot account for everything. There are always gaps or fissures, points at which language cannot signify. Its failure to explain everything is not the contingent failure of a particular symbolic order but a necessary failure inhering in symbolization itself. This failure creates the space for the subject to emerge and enjoy itself, but the failure of the symbolic order also troubles the subject and disturbs the stability of everyday life.

The failure of the symbolic order is not the fault of a lack of words. If anything, the English language proves that we have too many words for our experiences rather than not enough. The point is not that reality is too varied and multiple for words or that reality exceeds the words that we could use to describe it. Psychoanalytic theory insists rather that language fails through its production of an unavoidable antagonism. No matter how we symbolize reality, we always produce antagonisms that indicate a failure within the symbolic order. The nature of antagonism reveals that this failure is necessary rather than contingent. We can't hope one day to construct a perfect symbolic order free from antagonism, and this is reason for hope rather than despair. Though the necessity of antagonism is a barrier to utopia, it is also the seat of the subject's distance from symbolic constraint. The antagonism at once prevents the smooth functioning of the symbolic order and gives the subject of that order freedom in relation to it.

The fundamental antagonism that gives birth to psychoanalysis is the antagonism between the individual and the social order.[13] Freud's patients come to him because they are unable to endure the repression of desire that social life demands of them, and he views psychoanalysis as an attempt to assert the priority of individual desire in the face of an order that cannot accommodate it. The concern for this antagonism troubles Freud throughout his life. In *Civilization and Its Discontents*, which he writes near the end of his life, he returns to the idea that society is a bad bargain for the individual. He states, "We come upon a contention which is so astonishing that we must dwell upon it. This contention holds that what we call our civilization is largely responsible for our misery, and that we should be much happier if we gave it up and returned to primitive conditions."[14] Though Freud sees the catastrophe that civilization causes for the subject, he makes this call for a return to "primitive conditions" in jest. He recognizes that the subject only comes to exist through the social order that produces its suffering, which eliminates from the start the possibility of giving it up. In other words, there is no escape route through which one might avoid the antagonism, which means that antagonism is not mere opposition.

The difference between an opposition and an antagonism is crucial. When confronted with an opposition (like two teams playing a game against each other), one can just pick a side— root for the Chicago Bears rather than for the Dallas Cowboys. But an antagonism doesn't allow one this type of choice. If one chooses either side to the exclusion of the other, one loses both possibilities. It would be as if rooting for the Bears against the Cowboys caused the game to be canceled. Both sides of an antagonism are intertwined with each other, and this obviates a decisive choice for one side or the other.

The existence of real antagonism tells us that society cannot work out successfully. It will necessarily create discontents, not just among those who aren't successful but even among the most prosperous. Psychoanalysis emerges from the discontent of those whose material conditions suggest that they should be happy. It is the antagonism of the real that trips them up and dashes all plans for happiness, and perhaps it sends them into psychoanalysis. Antagonism is so central to the psychoanalytic project that a follower who abandons it ipso facto abandons the psychoanalytic project itself.

Translating antagonism into opposition is comforting, but it also eliminates the idea that the social order is inherently dysfunctional. Just as Freud throws Adler out of the Vienna Psychoanalytic Society for his deviation concerning the desiring subject, he breaks off relations with his would-be crown prince of psychoanalysis Carl Jung because Jung turns from the notion of antagonism to that of opposition. After initially siding with Freud, Jung comes to believe that the antagonisms that psychoanalysis uncovers—between, say, male and female sexuality—are just avatars of ancient mythic oppositions, like that of yin and yang. All of Jung's exploration of myth and symbolism stems from his flight from antagonism into opposition. Jung wants to embrace the opposition as constituting an overall wholeness rather than seeing it as an antagonism that prevents any such wholeness from emerging. With this move, he leaves the terrain of psychoanalysis, and Freud must break with him. For Jung, opposition characterizes the symbolic order, but it doesn't doom this order to failure. It is the source of its creativity and mystical power.[15]

For psychoanalysis, however, the real antagonism not only dooms every symbolic order to failure; it is also the condition of possibility for the symbolic order's existence. As a result of antagonism and the failure to become complete, the symbolic order accommodates new phenomena and new subjects. The adaptability of the symbolic order derives from the real that ultimately undermines it. One can see this relationship played out in the paradoxes of logic, which represent another form that the real takes on within the symbolic.

Like antagonism, the paradoxes of logic evince the necessary existence of the real within any symbolic order. These paradoxes show that the attempt to account for everything always runs aground. We can see this with the simple example of the barber paradox. According to this paradox, a barber shaves all men in the town who don't shave themselves, and those men only. The question that triggers the paradox then arises: Who shaves the barber? If the barber shaves himself, he shaves someone who shaves himself rather than only those who don't. But if the barber doesn't shave himself, he doesn't shave everyone who doesn't shave himself. Both possible answers prove incorrect. No matter how we try to resolve the problem, we keep running into the same impossibility. The paradox thus makes evident the inability of the symbolic order to solve all the problems that it produces.

When we think about the barber paradox, perhaps our head begins to hurt, but it doesn't seem inherently traumatic. Nonetheless, it should. All trauma has its basis in the logical impasses of the symbolic order like that of the barber paradox. The inability of the symbolic order to make sense of everything that it produces is traumatic. Trauma is the failure of sense—the encounter with non-sense. But this becomes clearer when we turn away from logic.

The trauma of the real becomes readily apparent when we consider social instances where the real manifests itself. It emerges whenever there is a hitch in the usual order of things. It occurs when a teacher is giving an account of something and a student asks a question that disturbs that account in a way that the teacher can't answer. The teacher's failure of mastery and evident discomfort is a trauma of the real. The symbolic authority reveals at this moment its lack of authority and the inability of the symbolic to cover everything. Or this trauma occurs when a child continues to ask why. At some point, the parent just says, "Because I said so." This is the real that interrupts the flow of the symbolic order.

Because the symbolic cannot account for the real, it has an impossible status within the symbolic order. The symbolic maps out all the possibilities that exist within its structure, and these possibilities govern the lives of the subjects living within these symbolic coordinates. But the symbolic also indicates—usually through omission—what is impossible. The real is impossible, and yet it occurs in spite of its impossibility. After a real event takes place, we readjust our symbolic system in order to account for the event and explain how it became possible, but prior to the event, it appears impossible.

Even though cinema displays images, it has the capacity to depict the impossible real. This is one of the great achievements of Sergei Eisenstein's *Battleship Potemkin* (1925). The film chronicles the revolt of sailors on the *Potemkin* and their success in overthrowing the despotic rule of the officers on the ship. Eisenstein's film stresses the impossibility of the sailors' collective act, but then it shows this act occurring. The film remains compelling today because it captures the impossible real in this way. Film's commitment to visualizing the real happening is one of the reasons for the medium's appeal. One cannot imagine a cinema that didn't touch on the real.

There are many examples of real events that were impossible according to the existing symbolic coordinates when they occurred: the slave revolt of Spartacus, the discovery of heliocentrism by Copernicus, Arnold Schönberg's invention of twelve-tone music, and so on. This was clearly the case with the collapse of the Soviet Union. Though retrospectively one can see the portents of this collapse, before it happened no one believed that it was possible. Even the Central Intelligence Agency (CIA) failed to predict it, and subjects on both sides of the Berlin Wall believed that nuclear destruction was much more likely than the fall of the Wall. The Soviet Union's collapse was impossible from the perspective of the Cold War symbolic structure. It seemed as if the division of the planet into the capitalist West and the communist East would endure as long as humanity itself endured. But then the situation changed radically, and the event that inaugurated the change has the status of real.

Though it seems tempting to differentiate between real impossibilities and the impossibilities of the real, between, say, the existence of a unicorn and the collapse of the Soviet Union, we should avoid this temptation. The existence of the real indicates to us that the impossible, in whatever form, is possible. We can draw the line between the truly impossible (the unicorn) and the possible impossible (the collapse of the Soviet Union) only from the side of the possible—that is to say, from the side of the symbolic order. The symbolic order constrains our sense of what is possible while at the same time trying to convince us that we are free to do whatever we want. The psychoanalytic conception of the real works in the opposite direction. It shows us that the impossible is always possible but that we can arrive at it only by grasping how narrowly our choices are constrained within the symbolic structure. We should not imagine that we can do anything but instead recognize our capacity for doing the impossible amid the antagonistic constraints that the symbolic order proffers.

# The imaginary

The real traumatizes the subject because it indicates the absence of a stable symbolic order that can provide a constant support for the subject's identity. The symbolic order does supply signification, but this signification doesn't support us as subjects in any substantial way. This is why we have recourse to the imaginary. The imaginary hides the real (or the incompletion of the symbolic) and thereby gives us a sense that our identity has a substantial foundation. The threat of the encounter with the real often triggers a retreat to the security of the imaginary and its promise of wholeness.

Lacan always insists that the imaginary plays a supplementary role to the symbolic order. We don't first go through the imaginary and then enter the symbolic, as if they represented stages on life's way. The imaginary doesn't have an independent status; it instead works to secure the rickety construction of the symbolic by giving it an image of wholeness that it doesn't have on its own. The real is symbolic impossibility, and the imaginary is the illusion of plenitude that hides this impossibility. It presents the subject with an abundance of choices, but none of the choices actually make a substantive difference. As long as the subject concerns itself with this imaginary plenitude, it misses the trauma of the real antagonism that disrupts every symbolic order.

Imaginary plenitude functions precisely like the cold medicine aisle at the grocery store. Everyone knows that there is no real cure for the common cold, and yet when we fall victim to a cold, we seek relief for our misery by going to seek a possible remedy. When we arrive at the cold medicine aisle, a plethora of choices confronts us. We can purchase a wide variety of brands and different types of each brand. The choices range from a Tylenol twelve-hour decongestant with pain reliever to a Sudafed four-hour antihistamine that doesn't cause drowsiness. An imaginary plenitude bombards the subject, and this plenitude creates the illusion that relief must really exist if we just make the correct choice. Imaginary plenitude is a haven for the subject who would otherwise confront real impossibility.

The impasse of a cure for the common cold acts in this example as a metaphor for a real antagonism. The plenitude of cold remedies translates this unsolved barrier into new terms that diffuse the effect of the failure. This is the function of the imaginary register in Lacan's system of thought, and in this precise sense the pun between imaginary number and imaginary order is not misleading. The real traumatizes the subject by stripping away any possible symbolic foundation for the subject's identity, and the imaginary plugs the leak. From the perspective of the imaginary, the world is whole, and identity is complete. But the wholeness that the imaginary provides is always illusory. Lacan's use of the term "imaginary" (*imaginaire* in French) relies on the term's double meaning: it is both a field of representation and an illusion.

It is easy to see how film can serve an imaginary function for the desiring subject. Sitting in the theater aware of myself as lacking, I look up at the screen and see Will Smith in *Men in Black* (Barry Sonnenfeld 1997), an image of overwhelming plenitude that enables me to forget temporarily my own lack. When cinema plays this role, it can have an ideological effect. Rather than change the social order, I imagine a better situation for myself through the cinematic star. The ineffectiveness of the symbolic order disappears on the screen. But this ideological effect is more or less benign. For too long, psychoanalytic film theorists inveighed against the imaginary seduction of the cinema, forgetting that the imaginary always points to a missing real.

The imaginary tries to convince us that the impossible real really is impossible and that the symbolic order has no fissures. There is a constant struggle taking place between the real and the imaginary in order to determine how we relate to the symbolic. The question is whether we will consider the symbolic order a fully constituted whole that successfully authorizes our identity or a self-divided semblance that constantly leads us into impasses that evince its failure. That is, will we view the symbolic from the perspective of the imaginary or from the perspective of the real?

The imaginary process of identification provides the subject a way to avoid recognizing itself as a desiring subject. Lacan theorizes imaginary identification as a short-circuiting of the path of desire. We identify with an image that we idealize—this is how imaginary identification functions—but desire subtends this process of identification. We use identification with the idealized image of the other in order to desire without confronting the trauma of real that desire involves. The image appears complete and not lacking, which distinguishes it from both the desiring subject and from desire's object.

# Desire

Desire in psychoanalytic terms is the result of lack. If we were complete, we would be completely satisfied and not seek something else. This lack is inherent in our condition as subjects; it is irremediable. As a result, it is impossible to cure subjects of lack and to achieve a harmonious wholeness. In contrast to other forms of therapy, psychoanalysis doesn't want to cure people of their lack but allow them to get over the idea that one can cure it and to embrace lack as constitutive rather than as an obstacle to overcome.

The precise name for lack in psychoanalysis is castration, which has always been a controversial term. Freud designates the castration complex as a dilemma that both sexes must confront, but he consigns castration itself only to women. One of Lacan's most important innovations is to reinterpret Freud's concept of castration in a symbolic sense. Castration, as Lacan understands it, is symbolic castration, which means simply that the subject is subjected to the signifier. As such, the subject must exist as a sexed being and not as a whole. Castration marks the way that the subject comes into being as a subject only through a cut that enables the subject to speak. The speaking being must be incomplete, and this incompleteness is castration.

Language divides the subject from itself by placing a layer of mediation within the subject's self-relation. I think of myself through words given to me by the Other. Language introduces a distance in the interior of the subject, and this division leaves the subject incapable of self-transparency. No speaking being can achieve self-transparency because when it speaks, it never knows fully what it's saying and always says more than it means to say. When the subject speaks, it speaks without consciously controlling every word, and this absence of total control allows the unconscious to intervene. The subject expresses its desire through what it doesn't mean to say.

The failure of the speaking being to coincide with itself becomes evident when one says, "I am I." The simple statement of identity does signify identity, but it simultaneously signifies difference through the existence of the two terms in the statement. The speaking subject must separate itself from itself in order to identify itself—Lacan refers to these two entities as the subject of the enunciation and the subject of the statement—and this necessity bespeaks the self-division of subjectivity along with the centrality of the unconscious for the subject.

When the individual enters into language, it loses its lost object and becomes a sexed subject. This constitutive loss produces desire because enjoyment is attached to this lost object. But at the same time, the lost object only exists insofar as it is lost. It has no substantial status and is not an empirical object that the subject actually gives up. Instead, the lost object is the product of our entrance into language. As we become speaking beings, we lose the object that we never had, and this loss creates the lost object that we associate a past time of plenitude, even though this time of plenitude never really existed. Plenitude is always imaginary. All nostalgia plays on this dynamic of subjectivity and partakes of its fundamental illusion.

Every desire, no matter how apparently idiosyncratic, is animated by the lost object. When we desire any particular empirical object, it functions as a stand-in for the primordially lost object that we can never find because it doesn't exist and has never existed. It is like the final solution to pi. There is no endpoint that will provide an ultimate answer, but a satisfaction resides in the desire itself.

Darren Aronofsky's debut film *Pi* (1998) enacts this form of satisfaction. It recounts the story of Max Cohen (Sean Gulette), who believes that his supercomputer has discovered a 216-digit number that will unlock various patterns in the world (like the stock market). But the film reveals that this solution coincides with a psychotic break: not only does Max's computer break down when spewing out the number but also Max himself undergoes a psychotic episode as he focuses on it. Aronofsky makes clear that the solution to a problem like pi doesn't reside in discovering a pattern to its irrationality but in the desire that this irrationality causes. Even though films move toward an end, they can—in the manner of Aronofsky's *Pi*—point back to the desire that moves without reference to an endpoint.

The problem is that as subjects of desire we don't desire to realize our desire and obtain the object. We desire instead to thwart our desire and thereby keep our desire going. All of the self-help books that exist in the world exist because we can't really help ourselves. Instead, we choose the path that will prevent us from fulfilling our desire, no matter how hard we try continuously to realize it. There is something in our desire that doesn't work and that prevents things from just working out for us.

The unconscious drives us to constantly undermine our conscious wishes, which are completely distinct from our unconscious desires. We are self-sabotaging beings. Even as modernity gives us the tools to achieve liberation from necessity and some degree of happiness, we work to destroy this possibility. Psychoanalysis emerges after modernity because it is only at this point, when many people are freed from necessity, that the self-sabotaging nature of human subjectivity becomes apparent. Because we are self-sabotaging beings, we cannot avoid the experience of trauma. Freud initially thinks that trauma is always an external event imposed on the subject— sexual abuse. This is known as the seduction theory, and Freud holds to it throughout most of the 1890s.

But then he comes to understand that in many cases the seduction was fantasized by the subject herself. This immediately provokes a couple of key questions: Why would someone do that? Why fantasize a trauma and not respite from trauma? The idea that the subject might fantasize a trauma goes against our entire way of conceiving desire and fantasy, and yet Freud insists on it. As he figures out, the fantasy of an external trauma relieves us from the dissatisfaction inherent in our own psychical processes. In this sense, an external trauma provides a degree of relief, and it inaugurates our being as desiring subjects.

The loss of the privileged object is at once the birth of the privileged object. We often hear people talk about the way that psychoanalysis privileges the attachment to the mother's breast, seeing this attachment as the perfect relationship that we want to return to after having lost it. But the breast only has this status—if it does at all—insofar as it is lost. It is the act of losing this object that gives it a privileged status. There is no experience of total satisfaction prior to the loss of this experience. It is only retroactively that an object becomes the lost object.

Some originary experience of traumatic loss constitutes us as subjects, even if this experience only occurs on the level of fantasy (because we never had the object in the first place). We then structure our lives around the idea of repeating the initial experience that itself never took place. We repeat a failure rather than a success. This is why one continues to encounter the same problems in each romantic partner or the same defects in a series of friends. We are always repeating, but we aren't repeating our successes. When we have a success, we forget about it and move on, but when we have a failure, the failure provides a point around which we organize our existence. We cherish our failures as moments that generate a lost object for us.

# The two objects

Psychoanalysis envisions two possible outcomes of desire aligned with its success and its failure. The subject can attempt to realize its desire by successfully obtaining the object, or it can satisfy its desire through the repeated failure to obtain the object. Ironically, the subject bent on successfully realizing its desire is doomed to failure, while the subject that embraces the necessity of failure can succeed. But this is a success of a different order than we're used to. After the emergence of psychoanalysis, we have to redefine success and failure: success involves sustaining ourselves in the absence of the object, and failure is the insistence on trying to obtain it.

One can never obtain the lost object, and if one does, one finds something other than the lost object. The lost object exists only insofar as it remains lost. Once we have an object, it becomes ordinary and we seek another object that might be the lost object. Even George Clooney becomes just an ordinary guy if one actually has a relationship with him. We cannot satisfy ourselves through having because having is precisely what destroys the desirability of the object.

In this sense, self-sabotage represents a desperate attempt to sustain desire. Manufacturing ways of not having the object keeps us desiring it. One of the ways that we do this is to place objects off-limits and make them sacred. We date the wrong kind of person for us; we overeat so that we'll feel bad and be able to desire having a good body; we overschedule our time so that we don't have the freedom that we desire; we drink too much so that we can desire feeling better or having more control. In each case, the obstacle to desire is more desirable for us than the supposed object that lies beyond this obstacle.

In order to make sense of this strange phenomenon, Lacan distinguishes between two types of object to which our desire relates. There is, for Lacan, an object of desire, which is the object through which the subject tries to realize its desire. This is what desire seeks. But there is also the lost object that causes the subject to desire, an object that Lacan christens the objet petit a or objet a.[16] In order to highlight this object's irreducibility to the signifier, Lacan insisted that translators leave it untranslated. It indicates the point of absence that arouses our desire because we associate it with a lost enjoyment that we are incapable of finding present anywhere in the world. No empirical object provides this enjoyment, but the objet a suggests its possibility to us.

The objet a takes on different forms. The objet a in the visual field is the gaze, and in the aural field it is the voice. These are the two forms of the object that Lacan adds to Freud's list of sexual objects. For Freud, the sexual objects correspond to phases of development, though their sexual charge lingers after the subject develops out of the various phases. The initial object is oral, the breast, and this is followed by excrement, the anal object. The phallic phase then arrives with the phallus as its object, and the different relations to the object, according to Freud, constitute sexual difference. Lacan does not view the objet a in terms of stages, and he focuses primarily on it as gaze and as voice.

The objet a is the lost object, but Lacan coins the term "objet a" rather than calling it the lost object (a term that

Freud employs) because he wants to avoid the suggestion that this object ever existed. The objet a becomes the cause of the subject's desire not because it once provided satisfaction for the subject but because it marks the loss that the subject experiences when it begins to speak. It is what the subject sacrifices of itself, but it has no substantial existence prior to its sacrifice, which is why the term "lost object" is somewhat of a misnomer.

The central point of Lacan's theoretical edifice—what he added not just to Freud but also to Hegel and the German Idealist tradition that he followed—is the objet a. Looking back on his intellectual trajectory, Lacan himself affirms this in his *Seminar XXI* when he states, "the *objet petit a* is perhaps what I had invented."[17] The objet a has such a crucial position because it enables us to think about the subject's relation to its world in terms of a lack that doesn't lack something substantial. It is not a present object that arouses our desire but what is missing in the field of experience. As such, the objet a is not the object of desire but the object that causes the subject to desire.

Every film utilizes the distinction between the objet a and the object of desire, but the distinction is perhaps clearest in Hitchcock's films. In the case of *The Birds* (1962), the object of the spectator's desire is a successful escape from the birds or the end of the threat that they pose. The objet a is actually the birds themselves. The bird attacks disrupt the idyllic scene at Bodega Bay, but this disruption fuels our desire as spectators. Hitchcock fully understands this, which is why he gives the spectator the birds' perspective on Bodega Bay just before they launch their most violent attack. This famous shot, which seems like a neutral look on the town and then becomes apparent as the birds' perspective, reveals the impossibility of a neutral look (or a look free from a subject's desire) while at the same time showing that the birds are the source of the disruption. A film like *The Birds* gives us the opportunity to turn briefly from the object of desire to the objet a, and it even preserves the disruptiveness of the objet a through its conclusion. This is a move that consciousness resists, and it requires the dreamlike quality of film to facilitate it.

We can think about the distinction between the object of desire and the objet a in another way, by considering our desire in relation to an ordinary object, like a can of Coke. When we approach a can of Coke, the Coke itself functions as the object of desire. We want to drink the soda and have no desire for the can that contains it. And yet, if there were a boundless supply of Coke in the world, we would have no desire for it. The cause of our desire for the Coke, the objet a in the case of the Coke, is the can that limits how much we can have. The objet a or object that causes our desire is not the object that we desire but the obstacle to that object.

Sometimes the obstacle is clearer. A can is only an obstacle to the quantity of Coke that we can drink, but the security gate prohibiting entry into an affluent neighborhood is a much more definite obstacle. The gate acts as an objet a and makes the affluent neighborhood into an object of desire. The houses in themselves require the gate—and locks on the doors—not just to keep others out but to render the dwelling desirable both for its inhabitants and for those excluded. Without the obstacle in some form, we would not desire to drink the Coke, live in the affluent neighborhood, or even have sex with attractive people. Their attractiveness is not desirable in itself but makes them desirable insofar as it places them outside of the realm of immediate accessibility.

It is only through the erection of the obstacle that the object of desire becomes desirable, which is why, for Lacan, the objet a has so much more importance than the object of desire. Through its function as an obstacle, the objet a can render any object desirable. Subjects desire indirectly via the obstacle rather than desiring the object directly. This understanding of desire indicates why the realization of desire doesn't bring satisfaction. Realizing our desire overcomes the obstacle, and the obstacle is the condition of possibility for the desire. The horrible dissatisfaction that accumulates with the accumulation of objects stems directly from the problem of the objet a and its difference from the object of desire. The obstacle is the manifestation of the lost object; it is how the lost object constitutes our desire. Losing the obstacle is always worse than losing the object of desire.

# Fantasy

The fact that the obstacle to our desire is its condition of possibility reveals the paradox of desire. Given this situation, any attempt to realize desire will necessarily end in catastrophe—the elimination of the desire that one realizes. The paradox of our desire—the closer we get to obtaining the object the more it recedes from us—necessitates a recourse to fantasy. The typical conception of fantasy focuses on the fact that fantasy enables us to realize our desire and to have the object that we can't have in reality, and fantasy does certainly play this role. I fantasize about having sex with Brad Pitt or Angelina Jolie—or both together—because I can't actually have either. Fantasy is a compensation for a failure in reality. We can succeed in fantasy where we otherwise couldn't. This function of fantasy is relatively innocuous: though it may inhibit us from acting to ameliorate our situation and foster contentment with the status quo, the fantasy of what we lack in reality doesn't necessarily lead us into political peril.

Fantasy also provides an image for the subject of what the Other desires, and this function is decidedly less benign. The subject confronts the Other's demand and must interpret the desire lying within this demand. The subject thus constantly asks itself, "What does the Other want?" This is an unanswerable question because there is no consistent and substantial Other that knows what it wants. Or to put it in other terms: the Other's desire is a mystery not only to the subject but also to the Other itself. Confronted with the enigma of the Other's desire, the subject resorts to fantasy in order to concoct a solution to this unanswerable question. Through fantasy, desire ceases to be fundamentally unanswerable and becomes a problem that one can solve.

When the subject fantasizes a solution to the Other's desire, one imagines that the Other has a consistent and substantial existence. This is the psychic and ultimately political danger that stems from this function of fantasy. It buttresses the dominance of social authority by granting this authority a substantiality that it doesn't actually have. The moment that I fantasize a solution to the Other's desire, I accept that the social authority knows what it's doing and therefore submit to the justification for its rule, even if I don't accede to the authority's demands. If we examine popularity in high school, this function of fantasy becomes quite clear.

The popular crowd represents the figure of the big Other in high school. Though these students don't technically rule the school, they have social authority, and everyone at the school would choose their good graces over the good graces of the principal. The subject who enters the high school confronts the desire of the Other in the form of the secret of popularity. Fantasy provides this subject a roadmap toward popularity and gaining the acceptance of the popular crowd. This roadmap tells one to wear particular clothes, speak with certain words, appreciate the proper music, like specific people, and so on. If the subject adheres to this fantasmatic roadmap, popularity seems assured. But the path is not so easy. The solution that fantasy provides to the desire of the Other is only an imaginary solution, and it assumes that the Other has a consistency that it doesn't have.

Though one may follow the fantasmatic roadmap to popularity perfectly, one might easily end up on the outside of the popular crowd. But the greater danger lies in actually achieving popularity. By doing so, one succumbs to the dominance of the social authority despite its lack of any real authority. The subject cedes itself to an Other that doesn't substantially exist. In this sense, fantasy is the vehicle for the conformism that characterizes not just subjects entering high school but subjects throughout the social order. We conform first on the level of fantasy, and from this moment forward, the existence of another possibility evaporates. This is how inegalitarian regimes perpetuate themselves. We fantasize the substantiality of the authority that these regimes proclaim for themselves. But despite this deleterious effect of fantasy's role in providing an imaginary solution for the desire of the Other, it is nonetheless not the most politically dangerous function of fantasy.

An even more politically dangerous function of fantasy is the transformation that it effects on the lost object. Fantasy enables us to imagine that we once had the lost object or objet a, that its loss is a contingent fact that we might remedy rather than the object's condition of possibility. Through a fantasy scenario, the subject stages having and losing the object, and some force or agent is always responsible for this loss. This is the problem. The subject turns its political energy against this agent that deprives the subject of its lost object.

In the case of Nazism, this phenomenon is clear. The Nazi's fantasy scenario depicts the Jew depriving Germany of its inner greatness through degeneration and corruption. The Final Solution follows directly from this fantasy scenario: by eliminating the Jew as such, the Nazis could recover the lost object and return Germany to its former greatness. The problem with this solution lies in its reliance on fantasy: no matter how many Jews the Nazis killed, they could never recover the lost object, which exists only insofar as it is lost. The Final Solution is more properly speaking the Unending Solution.

But Nazism doesn't have a monopoly on this political use of fantasy. Every time someone mentions the danger of immigration, the same phenomenon that gave rise to Nazism comes into play. The nationalist fantasy posits the immigrant as source of the loss that undermines the nation, and the elimination of immigrants becomes a pathway to restoring what the nation has lost, even though the nation, like the former Germany of the Nazis, has no former greatness to recover. Fantasy stages loss in order to convince subjects that they once had the lost object that they never had. In this way, it provides a narrative for explaining the absence that exists within every signifying structure.

The political danger of filmic fantasy manifests itself whenever a film tries to convince us that the lost object once existed and can be recovered. Perhaps the leading contemporary culprit purveying this type of fantasy is Quentin Tarantino, who makes films about recovering an identity that has been lost through oppression. His counterfactual revenge films, *Inglorious Basterds* (2009) and *Django Unchained* (2012), succumb fully to the temptation of fantasizing the lost object into existence. In this sense, we should align the films with the very systems they purport to criticize—Nazism and slavery— because they all employ the same form of self-justification. That is, the idea of the substantiality of the lost object undergirds Nazism, slavery, *Inglorious Basterds*, and *Django Unchained*. In the two films, Tarantino's heroes reclaim what Nazism and slavery took from them, avenge themselves on the criminal regimes, and thereby eliminate the traumatic loss. The problem with these films lies directly in the type of fantasy they proffer, a fantasy of the object's recovery. This fantasy is not, of course, confined to Tarantino's films but proliferates throughout the cinema. It is a commonplace of popular filmmaking.

At first glance, fantasy seems simply to repeat the function of the imaginary, but there is a slight, though significant, difference. While the imaginary obscures the absence within the symbolic order, fantasy explains its existence. Though this explanation blunts the trauma of the absence, it nonetheless acknowledges it and creates the possibility for an encounter with it, while no such possibility exists with the imaginary. As a result, the political valence of fantasy is never decided once and for all, unlike that of the imaginary, which is always ideological. Fantasy most often functions ideologically, but it can expose the failure of symbolic authority rather than shoring up that authority.

When fantasy emphasizes the loss of the object, it turns away from its ideological function. But in fact, all fantasy must focus to some extent on the object's loss. Trauma is where the subject's enjoyment resides, and fantasy provides a mode of access to that enjoyment. We fantasize in order to enjoy, but we don't recognize that the enjoyment produced by fantasy stems from the loss it depicts rather than in the act of obtaining the object. We believe in the supposed enjoyment of overcoming loss and miss how loss houses our enjoyment.

# Enjoyment

Though we are subjects of desire, enjoyment ultimately plays a determinative role for our being as subjects. If we can no longer find enjoyment in our lives or enjoy our desire, we will give up on life. Often, subjects bereft of enjoyment simply kill themselves. Even if we don't go this far, even though we might not resort to suicide, an overwhelming depression will overtake us, and we will become lifeless beings rather than vital subjects. Enjoyment is the sine qua non of our vitality.

The term "enjoyment" is a translation of Lacan's concept of jouissance.[18] Though jouissance takes on different guises throughout his intellectual trajectory, Lacan always insists on its fundamental status for the subject. In "The Subversion of the Subject and the Dialectic of Desire in the Freudian Unconscious," he writes, "It is Jouissance whose absence would render the universe vain."[19] We engage ourselves in existence through the enjoyment that this engagement provides for us. For psychoanalysis, there is no ultimate purpose of our actions in the world—in this sense, psychoanalysis agrees with existentialism—but enjoyment offers us a purpose in the absence of an ultimate one. As a result of our enjoyment, the universe is not vain for us. For psychoanalysis, enjoyment is the meaning of life. But this is far from the hedonistic philosophy that it seems to resemble. One can see the distinction between the psychoanalytic emphasis on enjoyment and hedonism by exploring the nature of enjoyment.

Just as we must distinguish between the object of desire and the object that causes desire, we must distinguish between pleasure and enjoyment. Enjoyment is not what we immediately assume, but neither is pleasure. From the beginning, Freud defines pleasure in a way that seems counterintuitive. For him, we experience pleasure through the elimination of excessive stimulation rather than through arousal. Though we might seek out stimulation (by, say, riding a roller coaster), the pleasure that we feel (during the ride) stems from this stimulation's disappearance (as the ride comes to a conclusion). As a result, the pleasure principle posits the elimination of stimulation as the guiding rule of the psyche.

Freud attaches pleasure to discharge. Thus, I feel pleasure when I relieve my pent-up sexual desire in a sex act, when I let my ideas out in speech after holding my tongue, when I dance wildly at a bar after sitting in my office cubicle all day, or when I urinate after allowing my bladder to fill to capacity. In each case, there is a clear pleasure involved in a literal or metaphorical discharge. Though the undeniable pleasure of eating appears at first to confound this schema, it actually fits well when one considers that eating is an elimination or discharge of hunger. When one is completely sated and has no more hunger, eating ceases to be pleasurable, which is why one must force oneself to vomit if one is to continue this form of pleasure unabated. But even considering the role that vomiting might play in the pleasure of eating calls the apparent simplicity of pleasure into question. If I make myself vomit in order to be able to eat more, I have left the domain of pleasure, just as Freud himself would toward the end of his life.

When Freud wrote *Beyond the Pleasure Principle* in 1920, he conceives of what he calls the death drive for the first time. The death drive is a structure that controls the subject beyond the pleasure principle. It overrules the power of the pleasure principle and leads the subject to seek suffering rather than pleasure. At the same time, this turn in Freud's thought makes theoretical space for what Lacan would later term jouissance or enjoyment. One can only think about the possibility of enjoyment if the pleasure principle does not have the last word, and this dethroning of the pleasure principle occurs in Freud's

1920 work. As much as the discovery of the unconscious at the beginning of psychoanalysis, it represents a decisive moment for psychoanalytic theory.

The difference between pleasure and enjoyment lies in the inherent excessiveness of the latter. The term "excessive enjoyment" is a redundancy because enjoyment is by definition excessive. When one enjoys, one necessarily enjoys too much. Enjoyment is too much pleasure, and as such, it always involves suffering. Subjects necessarily suffer their enjoyment. Pleasure does not disturb us, but enjoyment derails our subjectivity at the same time as it gives the subject a reason to keep going. Enjoyment disturbs our happiness and deprives us of pleasure, but we pursue it nonetheless. It is what goes against our own good and against our self-interest. We derive enjoyment from sacrificing our self-interest rather than pursuing it.

Enjoyment rules the cinema. Though minimalist films that try to downplay the spectator's enjoyment certainly exist, film is inherently an excessive art. It aims at bombarding the spectator with more than she or he can process. Even films that show and say little provide an excess for the spectator. We shouldn't be surprised that studios and filmmakers constantly seek to make cinema ever more excessive. They add sound, color, wide-screen formats, Sensurround, Smell-O-Vision, IMAX, THX, 3-D, and so on. These excesses are not betrayals of the cinematic art but the logical extension of its excessiveness. The enjoyment that cinema provides leads to cinephilia or addiction, just as heroin or any other substance that proffers enjoyment. Though it might not have the destructive effects of a drug, cinema nonetheless gets in the way of the subject pursuing its good.

As opposed to pleasure, enjoyment depends on its opposition to the good and to self-interest. That is to say, we enjoy wasteful and useless activities. The enjoyment attached to drunkenness is not simply the absence of restraint that it allows but also the freedom from utility that it authorizes. When drunk, I can act uselessly, and I almost inevitably do. But the inutility of enjoyment is not purely pleasurable. Enjoyment is always traumatic enjoyment. Though we don't enjoy every trauma, we never enjoy without trauma.

Enjoyment has a self-destructive or sacrificial structure to it because our enjoyment is tied to the lost object, which exists only through its loss. In this sense, enjoyment is inextricable from loss, and there is no enjoyment without loss. Our self-destructiveness is not a pointless activity that we might remedy. It instead constitutes the basis for our capacity to enjoy. Through self-sacrifice, we create loss that we enjoy. This is one of the most important insights of psychoanalysis but also one of the most difficult to accept.

## Screen theory

When psychoanalytic film theory first emerges in earnest, enjoyment plays no part in it, and this should serve as an important clue as to how off base this initial theory was. For the psychoanalytic film theory of the 1970s and 1980s, the imaginary serves as the privileged category for the analysis of cinema. On one level, this makes sense insofar as the cinema itself relies on a series of images. But the imaginary is also the least important of Lacan's three registers, the register that he spends the least amount of time talking about. To the extent that it relies on the imaginary to the exclusion of the traumatic real and enjoyment, psychoanalytic film theory starts off on the wrong foot.

The first historically significant attempt to develop a psycho-analytic film theory occurs in France. Influenced by the thought of both Freud and Lacan, thinkers such as Jean-Louis Baudry, Jean-Pierre Oudart, and Christian Metz advance a way of thinking about the cinema that focuses on specific effects of the spectator's situation in the cinema. They link the effects of the cinema on the spectator to particular psychoanalytic concepts.

In each case, the central psychoanalytic concept is different, which means that each theorist creates a particular type of film theory, but the reception of these theories tends to blend them together. Baudry conceives of the cinematic apparatus as placing the spectator in the position of the infant in Lacan's mirror stage. Oudart sees the concept of suture—the relationship of the subject to the system of signifiers—at work in certain uses of the shot/reverse shot technique in the cinema. And Metz, employing two terms from Lacan's conceptual framework, theorizes that the underlying form of cinema hides its underlying symbolic structure. Two ideas—the screen functioning as a mirror for the subject and the film suturing the subject into its signifying order—emerge as the primary takeaway from this initial burst of theorizing, and this amalgam manifests itself most prominently not in France but in Great Britain.

In the 1970s, the film journal *Screen* becomes the home where several exponents of this type of psychoanalytic approach to cinema publish essays. In fact, the journal functions as such a crucial site for the dissemination of this theory that the theory itself is known in many circles as Screen theory. Today, one employs the term "Screen theory" in order to distinguish this particular form of psychoanalytic theorizing about the cinema from later manifestations in the 1990s and 2000s that hewed much more closely to Freud and Lacan's own thought. The three principal figures in the development of Screen theory are Laura Mulvey, Stephen Heath, and Colin MacCabe, but it is Laura Mulvey who publishes what most perceive as the ultimate text of Screen theory. Her "Visual Pleasure and Narrative Cinema" turns psychoanalysis toward feminist ends, and it does so by taking Lacan's essay "The Mirror Stage as Formative of the *I* Function" as its point of departure.[20] Screen theory on the whole views popular cinema as a grave political danger, precisely because, as Baudry and Metz notice, it tends to hide the act of production as it immerses spectators in a bath of images.

Two essays, one by Lacan and one by his disciple (and son-in-law) Jacques-Alain Miller, serve as the chief inspiration for Screen theory. From Lacan's "Mirror Stage" essay, Screen theory adopts the idea that the fragmented body becomes an ego when it misrecognizes itself as a whole by identifying with its mirror image, and the theory translates this idea into the situation of cinematic spectatorship. From Miller's "Suture

(Elements of the Logic of the Signifier)," Screen theory takes up the concept of suture and transforms it into the ideological function performed through popular cinematic form.[21] In both cases, a thoroughgoing misreading of the psychoanalytic concept leads to the development of a film theory that has little to do with the psychoanalytic thought that gave birth to it. What passes for Lacanian film theory bears no real resemblance to Lacan.

In the first place, Lacan's essay on the mirror stage plays a minuscule role in his overall psychoanalytic theory. He wrote the essay in 1949, before he began the seminars in which he developed his thought, and its origins actually date back to the late 1930s, when he first proposed the concept. Even as early as 1954 during his *Seminar II*, Lacan announces that he himself finds the mirror stage a dated concept. And his discovery of the objet a as the nodal point of his theory of desire in 1962 leads him to emphasize that this object is precisely what eludes the mirror image.[22] The problem with the idea of the mirror stage is that it leads to an emphasis on the imaginary at the expense of the real, which is why Screen theory's focus on this essay leads to a dead end.

But even within the confines of the mirror stage essay itself, Screen theory performs a butchered operation on Lacan's concept. According to Lacan, the infant between the ages of six and eighteen months has a fragmented experience of its body and has yet to develop an ego. At some point during this period, however, the infant looks in a mirror and sees a whole being instead of a fragmentary one. This deception, as Lacan sees it, is essential to the function of the imaginary order, which has the effect of creating illusory wholeness. The crowning achievement of the imaginary order is the subject's ego, but in this essay and throughout his career, Lacan emphasizes that though the ego is a bodily ego, it is imaginary in both senses of the term—an illusion and an image. The aim of the mirror stage essay is accounting for the formation of the ego through a process of imaginary identification.

The mirror stage has nothing to do with the production of a subject, but this is how Screen theory interprets and deploys the essay. The primary theorist who takes up this essay is Jean-Louis Baudry, who writes two influential articles entitled "Ideological Effects of the Basic Cinematic Apparatus" and "The Apparatus: Metapsychological Approaches to the Impression of Reality in Cinema." Baudry aligns his critique of the cinema with his reading of the "Mirror Stage" essay: both structures give an identification to the individual and in doing so hide the production process that engenders that identity. By rendering production invisible, Baudry argues, the cinematic apparatus deceives us about our own status in relation to the image. Though we are immobile and passive, we identify with the camera and experience a sense of mastery over the visual field through this identification. In Baudry's view, the apparatus also convinces us that we belong to the world of the visual field. In this way, it obscures the spectator's alienation from what she or he sees.

As Screen theory sees it, the belonging that the apparatus produces is ideological interpellation. Ideology enables individuals to believe that they are subjects—to believe that they can determine their own lives, that socioeconomic factors are not controlling them, and that they do not belong to any particular class or have any definite bond with others in their class. Ideological interpellation gives an individual a sense of identity and direction so that questioning about the social order as a whole and its injustice doesn't arise. This process works more powerfully in the cinema than anywhere else in society, according to Baudry. In the cinema, one can gain a sense of identity through the act of seeing heroic figures on the screen. I see Sandra Bullock or Denzel Washington acting in a specific way, and I model myself on them. The filmic screen functions like a mirror. This enables me to gain the illusion of subjectivity and the sense of belonging that comes with that subjectivity.

For Lacan, the subject misrecognizes itself in the form of an ego through the mirror stage, and in this sense, the mirror stage represents a turn away from subjectivity rather than the constitution of it. But for Screen theory, the outcome of the mirror stage is not the ego but the subject that conceives itself as the master of what it sees. The difference is not simply terminological. Though Lacan does theorize the emergence of a false sense of mastery in the mirror stage, that mastery concerns the body itself and not the entire visual field. The child that sees itself in the mirror imagines that it has mastery over its body, not that it has mastery over everything that it sees. Much more importantly, Screen theory's transformation from ego to subject has the catastrophic effect of eliminating the actual psychoanalytic subject, which is what doesn't fit into the social order in Lacan's theory, from the account. Screen theory contends that the mirror stage as it plays out in film spectatorship produces the subject as its ideological effect. As a result, popular spectatorship is a political nightmare from which Screen theorists dream of emancipating us. But this is a nightmare of their own creation that has nothing to do with actual psychoanalytic theory or actual spectatorship.

Through the focus on the mirror stage, Screen theory develops a critique of what it calls the cinematic gaze, which it identifies with the camera. The gaze assists in the ideological production of the spectator as a subject, according to this theory, because it provides an illusory sense of mastery over the visual field. Via the camera, the spectator becomes the master of all it surveys, and in the process, the spectator becomes blind to her or his real dependence.

Laura Mulvey gives this notion of the gaze its most famous turn when she employs it to feminist ends. Her essay "Visual Pleasure and Narrative Cinema" not only marks a major contribution to Screen theory; it has become by far the most widely anthologized essay in the history of film studies. Mulvey's thesis is that Hollywood cinema deploys the gaze in order to transform the female character in film into a spectacle who exists just to be voyeuristically seen. She writes,

> In a world ordered by sexual imbalance, pleasure in looking has been split between active/male and passive/female. The determining male gaze projects its phantasy onto the female figure, which is styled accordingly. In their traditional exhibitionist role women are simultaneously looked at and

displayed, with their appearance coded for strong visual and erotic impact so that they can be said to connote *to-be-looked-at-ness*.[23]

The camera and the male character work in concert with the spectator to take up the gaze, while the female character embodies only "to-be-looked-at-ness." The gaze represents the enemy that Screen theory must struggle against, even if this enemy is impossible to eliminate once and for all.

Mulvey builds her conception of the gaze on the basis of Lacan's mirror stage essay, which plays the same role for her as it does for Baudry. The look of the male spectator at the female on the screen is akin to the look of the infant into the mirror. During this gaze, the fragmentary body of the infant takes on the illusion of wholeness at the cost of distorting the object being seen. Mulvey focuses on the violence of the gaze on the object, whereas Baudry inveighs against the danger for the spectator who looks and then adopts the position of a subject. In both cases, however, the gaze functions as the cinematic vehicle for ideology, and it thus demands a ruthless critique. This is probably the most fateful development in the history of Screen theory. In the foundation of his thought, Lacan doesn't align vision with a look of mastery as Screen theory does but instead focuses on what disrupts our mastery when we look. Here, the misunderstanding is complete.

But incredibly, the errors that occur with the concept of suture are just as grave. In "Suture," Miller explains Lacan's conception of subjectivity through a reference to Gottlob Frege's theory of number. He compares the role that the subject plays within the system of signification to the role that the number 0 plays in Frege's theory. According to Miller, suture shows that the symbolic is not a closed system but one whose internal structure demands a reference to what is outside it. Suture marks the point at which the externality of the subject manifests itself within the signifying system, and it thus testifies to the system's necessary lack of completion or wholeness. The subject is what doesn't fit, not what does.

When Jean-Pierre Oudart imports the concept of suture to the analysis of cinema, he retains some of Miller's original sense. In "Cinema and Suture," Oudart credits Robert Bresson with discovering suture in the cinema in his film *Procès de Jeanne d'Arc* (*The Trial of Joan of Arc*, 1962).[24] According to Oudart, Bresson uses editing—specifically shot/reverse shot technique—to locate the spectator within the filmic space, and Oudart celebrates Bresson for his employment of suture. For Oudart (at least in his essay "Cinema and Suture"), there is no inherent ideological effect to suture, but this is precisely the unhappy conclusion that the concept comes to as Screen theory transforms it.

During the 1970s and 1980s, suture becomes the ubiquitous term for the subject's ideological interpellation into the illusory reality of the cinema. Rather than being a concept that indicates the incompleteness of the signifying system, suture comes to signify the wholeness of this system. The point at which the film sutures the spectator is the point at which the subject succumbs to the ideological power of the filmic text. The term "suture" grows into shorthand for narrative cinema's ideological functioning.

Daniel Dayan is the theorist most responsible for this transformation. In an often-anthologized essay entitled "The Tutor-Code of Classical Cinema," Dayan associates suture with cinema's ideological function in no uncertain terms. He concludes the essay with a thoroughgoing indictment of suture. He writes, "By means of the suture, the film-discourse presents itself as a product without a producer, a discourse without an origin. It speaks. Who speaks? Things speak for themselves and of course, they tell the truth. Classical cinema establishes itself as the ventriloquist of ideology."[25] From Dayan's perspective, psychoanalytic theory can assist us in understanding the ideological role that cinema plays in the social order.

This conception of psychoanalysis explains how we fit smoothly into the social order and mistakenly take this order's presentation of reality for reality as such. The problem is that psychoanalysis emerges out of the subject's inability to fit smoothly into the social order. As Miller originally articulates it, suture stands for the subject's inherent externality vis-à-vis the symbolic order and the disruptive mark that the subject leaves on this order. But this disruptiveness disappears as psychoanalytic theory becomes psychoanalytic film theory.

The problem is not that psychoanalytic film theory diagnoses cinema as ideology but that it performs this diagnosis much too abruptly and without adequate recourse to psychoanalysis itself. One could easily make this diagnosis without discussing psychoanalysis at all, by simply lamenting the role that power plays in cinematic spectatorship and indicting cinema for its creation of a reality effect. Screen theory doesn't need to discuss psychoanalysis in order to criticize popular cinema in the very way that it does. That is to say, nothing would be changed except the terminology if one subtracted psychoanalysis from Screen theory.

But the emergence of Screen theory had the effect of preventing the development of a genuine psychoanalytic film theory. Film critics imagined that they already knew how psychoanalysis could be brought to bear on the cinema, so they didn't need to think further about this relationship. They could continue to adhere to or attack Screen theory as if it were the manifestation of a psychoanalytic approach to the cinema. And they could be deaf to the articulation of a compelling alternative.

# The trauma of Joan Copjec

Throughout the 1970s and the early 1980s, Screen theory enjoyed an unchallenged reign as the embodiment of psychoanalytic film theory. Though many questioned its tenets, no one disputed the psychoanalytic credentials of Screen theory. The first inroad against the dominance of Screen theory comes in 1986, with the publication of Jacqueline Rose's *Sexuality in the Field of Vision*. In this work,

Rose explicitly questions the emphasis that Screen theory places on the mirror stage and imaginary identification in spectatorship.[26] But Rose's most important contribution is her critique of the conceptualization of the gaze. Rose provides a sophisticated account of the gaze as a form of the objet a, but she doesn't emphasize the status of the gaze as real rather than symbolic or imaginary in her critique. This is what Joan Copjec stresses in much detail in her groundbreaking 1989 essay "The Orthopsychic Subject."[27]

From the beginning, it is important to distinguish the gaze from the look. Though Lacan, writing in French, cannot make this distinction—*le regard* means both "look" and "gaze"—the two terms in English allow for an important clarification. The look is the subjective activity of seeing, while the gaze is the objet a within the field of vision that the look cannot see. It is important, after Copjec's intervention, always to maintain the distinction between the look that surveys the visual field and the gaze as objet a within the visual field. There is no look that can see the gaze, but there is no look without the gaze that it cannot see.

According to Copjec, film confronts the subject with a real absence that remains irreducible to any imaginary or symbolic identification, and it is this absence that acts as the cause of the subject's desire. The absence is the gaze. In "The Orthopsychic Subject," she states, "The subject is the effect of the impossibility of seeing what is lacking in the representation, what the subject, therefore, wants to see. Desire, in other words, the desire of representation, institutes the subject in the visible field."[28] That is to say, the subject emerges through the point of impossibility. The essence of the cinematic situation lies not in what the subject sees but the absence or gaze within the visual field that it surveys. The gaze as real, not imaginary plenitude, has the determinative role in the spectator's relationship to the visual field.

Copjec's essay introduces Lacan's category of the real into a psychoanalytic film theory obsessed with the imaginary and symbolic orders. It is not by accident that the title of Christian

Metz's foundational work of psychoanalytic film theory, *The Imaginary Signifier*, references the imaginary and the symbolic but not the real. Screen theory concerns itself with how the imaginary situation of cinema spectatorship furthers the ideological structure operating within the symbolic order. Because Screen theory views cinema almost entirely through the lens of the imaginary, it never grasps the real absences that haunt all spectatorship. This is where Copjec intervenes.

In her analysis of Screen theory, Copjec identifies the manifestation of its avoidance of the real—a preoccupation with power at the expense of desire. Like the psychoanalytic apostate Alfred Adler, Screen theorists take refuge in a theory of power that completely ignores the desire that draws spectators into the cinema in the first place. Cinema, for these theorists, concerns the power of the apparatus over the spectator and the power of the male over the female. In this sense, Copjec argues, Screen theory is much more aligned with the thought of Michel Foucault than that of Jacques Lacan, and it fails to recognize how power fails to account for the disruptiveness of the real in cinematic spectatorship.

The real, for Lacan, is always traumatic, and it is thus entirely appropriate that Copjec's essay that privileges the real had a traumatic effect on some of the original exponents of Screen theory themselves. At a conference entitled "Théorie du Cinéma et Crise dans la Théorie" in Paris in 1988, Copjec presented the paper that eventually became "The Orthopsychic Subject" for the first time to respondents that included Christian Metz and Raymond Bellour, two of the giants of the ruling version of psychoanalytic film theory at the time. Both Metz and Bellour verbalized their disagreement with Copjec, but Bellour, who was asked to write an official response for the journal issue produced from the conference, registered the traumatic impact of Copjec's essay in writing.[29]

Though Bellour agreed to write an essay in response to Copjec, he found her argument so out of bounds that he changed his mind. Instead of an essay, he wrote a letter to the journal explaining why he couldn't write a response. In this brief letter, he contends that Copjec failed to appreciate the genuine contributions of both French and American psychoanalytic film theorists and, what's more, she failed to follow "the rules of the game."[30] Bellour's outrage is not misplaced: it stems directly from Copjec's claim that Bellour and other Screen theorists based their theorizing on an incorrect understanding of Lacan's thought. In his letter, Bellour assails Copjec's presumption in making this claim. He writes that her text "lets one believe that they [the Screen theorists] would all be incorrect in relation to a hypothetical truth of Lacan of which it [Copjec's text] would be the possessor." He then labels the essay "an extreme and personal reaction."[31] If Bellour believed that Copjec's had only a "hypothetical truth of Lacan," we might imagine that he would have written an essay correcting her rather than writing a letter dismissing her. The existence of the letter in place of the essay is an absence indicative of a trauma. What Bellour cannot say signifies more emphatically than what he does say. But Bellour's immediate (lack of a) reaction to "The Orthopsychic Subject" is only the beginning of a profound deafness that lasts well into the 2000s. Though critics acknowledge the existence of Copjec's essay, no one engages with it until twenty years after its publication.

At a certain point, it becomes clear that film critics hang on to Screen theory and ignore Copjec's intervention because it offers easier fodder for critique. This is surely the case with David Bordwell, who is the coeditor of *Post-Theory*, an attack on psychoanalytic film theory for its dominance of the field and its de facto suppression of empirical and historical research. In his essay in the volume, Bordwell spends time criticizing Copjec as an exemplar of the "associationist reasoning of contemporary film theory," grouping her with the very theorists whom Copjec herself attacks in her essay.[32]

What stands out in Bordwell's critique of Copjec, however, is that he targets her analysis of detective fiction and film noir rather than her revision of psychoanalytic film theory. Clearly, Bordwell is acquainted with Copjec (since he writes about her for a number of pages), but he ignores her signal contribution to film theory. In order to sustain his assault on what he calls "subject-position theory" and "culturalism" in film studies, Bordwell must omit the one theory that fits within neither camp and that would therefore throw a wrench in his attack plan—the psychoanalytic film theory that Copjec articulates in "The Orthopsychic Subject." The existence of this essay continues to signify because almost everyone is aware of it and yet almost no one pays attention to it.

# The significance of Slavoj Žižek

If silence met Joan Copjec's critique of Screen theory, the same is not the case for Slavoj Žižek. Though Žižek does not often take on Screen theory in the direct manner that Copjec does in her essay, he makes a definitive case for a Lacan of the real and the importance of this Lacan for the understanding of film.[33] The sheer volume of Žižek's theoretical production—he has averaged over a book per year since his first book in English appeared in 1989—demands critical engagement, if not appreciation. Not only does Žižek produce a great quantity of theoretical material, his dramatic style and provocative pronouncements garner him considerable attention as well. He is largely responsible for instantiating the genuine psychoanalytic film theory that Copjec initiated.

Žižek's interpretation of Lacan in *The Sublime Object of Ideology* in 1989 changes the common conception of him as a thinker. Rather than accepting the traditional grouping of Lacan with other French theorists like Jacques Derrida, Gilles Deleuze, Michel Foucault, and Roland Barthes, Žižek links Lacan to figures in the history of philosophy such as Descartes, Kant, and Hegel. In doing so, he establishes Lacan as a philosopher of the subject rather than a critic of subjectivity. This shift leads to Žižek's implicit critique of Screen theory's entire project, which is based on the belief that the subject is an effect of ideology.

Where Screen theory criticizes popular cinema for producing the subject as an ideological effect, Žižek criticizes cinema when it obscures the trauma of subjectivity through the deployment of an ideological fantasy. Subjectivity, as Žižek sees it, is what emerges out of the failure of ideological interpellation, not the result of a successful interpellation. The subject is thus not ideological but a form of resistance to ideology. It is not identical with the ego, which is the product of an imaginary misrecognition. The subject is the subject of the signifier, so it depends initially on the signifier and on ideology. But the signifier produces a subject divided from itself, and this division is the key to its ability to contest ideology. The unconscious is not just ideology but also the source of real opposition to ideology. Though cinema can obscure this possible opposition to ideology, it can also reveal it by engaging the spectator with the way in which the subject appears in the cinematic fiction as a gap within the fiction.

There is a potential for exploding ideology in the cinema that exists because for Žižek films have the status of dreams. Žižek follows Freud and Lacan in viewing the dream (and thus the film) as a privileged site for the subject's encounter with its desire. In *The Sublime Object of Ideology*, Žižek proclaims, "It is only in the dream that we come close to the real awakening—that is, to the Real of our desire."[34] Due to its structure as visual fiction, cinema engages the real that everyday life leaves hidden.

Žižek's filmic analyses almost always focus on certain pivotal scenes in which film manages to trap and expose the spectator's desire rather than on entire films. Often, these are not the scenes that other critics celebrate but rather ones that appear inconsequential. But Žižek's analysis shows how the encounter with our desire happens when we least expect it. For instance, in his discussion of Alfred Hitchcock's *Psycho* (1960), Žižek doesn't focus on the celebrated shower scene but what follows after it. One of the most important scenes in the history of cinema for Žižek involves Norman (Anthony Perkins) hiding the car of the just-murdered Marion (Janet Leigh) in the swamp behind the Bates Motel.

The real of desire is not present in the spectator's or Norman's look at Marion in the shower but in the object sinking—or failing to sink—in the swamp. When Hitchcock shows that the car stops sinking midway through its descent, he highlights the spectator's desire and aligns that desire with Norman's cover-up of a murder. He cuts to Norman's anxious face and thereby encourages the spectator to share Norman's desire for the car to sink. Žižek points out that the filming of this scene exposes the spectator's investment in the film through desire and the impossibility of an impartial view of the events on the screen. The sequence forces the spectator to confront her or his complicity with Norman's action on the level of desire. Hitchcock deprives the spectator of the illusion of psychic distance from what transpires within the diegetic reality, and this signals the radicality of the film.

Despite Žižek's constant reference to film, many film theorists view him as a philosopher lacking any genuine concern for film as such. According to this critique, films simply serve as examples for Žižek, and his real concern lies with the theoretical point that the film exemplifies. According to Stephen Heath, "It is indicative that Zizek has, in fact, little to say about 'institution,' 'apparatus,' and so on, all the concerns of the immediately preceding attempts to think cinema and psychoanalysis (films and novels will thus mostly be referred to without any particular distinction between them as forms)."[35] Vicky Lebeau echoes this point, contending that "it is the specificity of cinema that seems to go missing in Žižek's account—the connivance between spectacle and image, projection and narrative."[36] It is the case that Žižek doesn't often provide sustained analysis of entire films, and his analyses sometimes ignore formal aspects of the films that he discusses. But nonetheless, this line of thought misses the weight of Žižek's contribution.

The critique overlooks the many occasions where Žižek directly analyzes form, such as his interpretation of the deployment of the spectator's desire in relation to form in *Psycho*. But more importantly, it fails to acknowledge that Žižek's very turn to film evinces an appreciation of its specificity. He returns to filmic examples more than any other because film speaks in a specific way to contemporary desire. The specificity of film for Žižek lies in how it stages our desire. Filmic fictions have the ability to confront us with the desire that we would otherwise miss.

Though Žižek doesn't emphasize film form to the extent that Copjec does or develop a fully worked out system of film interpretation, his brief analyses of important film scenes help to pave the way for other psychoanalytic theorists who have followed in Žižek's wake.[37] In the face of the complete dominance of the old concept of the gaze elaborated by Screen theory in the 1970s and 1980s, the theoretical transformation that Žižek led has been revolutionary. However brief or merely exemplary his filmic analyses have been, they have played a central part in the rebirth of psychoanalytic film theory.

## The gaze or what is not seen

The turn from Screen theory to a genuine psychoanalytic film theory involves a radical change of emphasis in cinematic analysis. Screen theory prioritizes the process of imaginary identification that takes place when a spectator watches a film, whereas psychoanalytic film theory focuses on the way that a film relates to the spectator's desire. This is not simply a minor adjustment but a wholesale theoretical shift in which nothing remains the same. The approach to particular films does not begin with the illusion of plenitude in the image and the absent production process that this imaginary plenitude obfuscates, as Screen theory's approach does. Instead, it focuses on how the film formally structures the relationship between plenitude and absence within the image. It discovers the political bearing of a film by examining how the film deploys plenitude and absence, and the result is that the politics of cinema become much more complex.

One of the great ironies in the history of film theory is the very term "Screen theory." We could correctly say that the theorists associated with the journal *Screen* deny the existence of a screen. For them, as Joan Copjec points out in "The Orthopsychic Subject" (and subsequently in *Read My Desire*), the cinema screen functions like a mirror. The problem with this reduction of the screen to the mirror is that the screen doesn't just reflect an imaginary ideal ego back to the spectator. It also produces an encounter with what Lacan calls the real, the point of impossibility within the symbolic structure. As Lacan himself states in *Seminar XIII*, "The screen is not only what hides the real—it is surely that—but at the same time, it indicates it."[38] In the visual field, the screen serves a double function: it is a site for presenting the image and for marking what lacks within the image.

When discussing the screen, Lacan uses the French term *écran*, which has the same contradictory significance as the English word "screen." A screen is simultaneously a device that enables one to see images and an obstacle to seeing. One looks at a movie screen and sees images on the screen, but a screen in front of someone prevents one from seeing her or him. Lacan's conception of the screen is paradoxical: it "hides the real" when it functions as a site for seeing, but it "indicates" the real through its act of blocking what the subject can see.

The screen does not reflect the subject's idealized image back to it but rather carves out a hole in the field of vision. This hole disturbs the subject's look; the screen reveals to the subject that it is not all-seeing, that there is no such thing as a God's eye view on reality. But the disturbance of the subject's vision is the condition of visibility for the field that the subject sees. Without what the subject cannot see, it would not see anything at all. The screen that provides us something to look at simultaneously screens off a portion of what we can see, which is precisely the act of representation itself. The act of representation appears within the representation as representation's internal limit. No representation can show itself showing or reveal itself revealing, and the screen marks this limit. But the limit is a productive limit.

The blank spot within the field of vision that the screen produces engages the desire of the subject in this field. An all-seeing subject would have no desire to look, which is why nudist colonies are not hotbeds of desire but instead paradigms for desire's evacuation. We desire to see because we can't see everything, and the barrier to our seeing functions as the object-cause of our desire or objet a in the visual field. This is the version of the objet a that Lacan calls the gaze.

The gaze is a distortion within the visual field, a point at which the seeming omnipotence of vision breaks down. In this sense, it is the reverse of the mastering look criticizing by Screen theory. It appears in the guise of a blot that renders a portion of the visual field unintelligible. This distortion is not simply a contingent aspect of the visual field, an aspect that might be there or not. Without it, there would be nothing to see, even though the subject seldom notices the gaze when it looks. The gaze defines the visual field through the distortion that it creates, but most of the time, it remains difficult to detect even as it motivates the subject's act of seeing. The virtue of the cinema is that it can render this distortion apparent.

Lacan's privileged example of the gaze occurs not in the cinema but in painting. He sees it at work in Hans Holbein's *The Ambassadors*, a painting that depicts a pair of wealthy world travelers with the accoutrements of their voyages surrounding them in the image. But at the bottom of the picture in front of these world travelers, the spectator can see a large though obscure figure. While looking at the painting from the front, this figure looks like a blot that has no place in the world of wealth and splendor depicted in the painting. Perhaps it appears as a mistake that the painter made. It is only when one approaches the painting and looks down at this figure from the top right that one can decipher that it is actually a skull. Holbein's use of the technique of anamorphosis elongates the image of the skull and requires a certain angle of spectatorship to compress it into an intelligible figure. One can see the skull only from this extreme angle of spectatorship, and the anamorphic distortion enables spectators to encounter the gaze. Spectators can see the distorted skull only through the act of involving themselves within the painting by moving forward and looking from an unusual angle.

When the skull becomes visible, the spectator recognizes her or his own involvement in the picture. That is to say, the gaze reveals that Holbein did not just paint the picture for a neutral or impartial look. One must move to a particular perspective to see it, revealing that the position of the spectator counts within the painting. The painting itself takes the spectator's desire into account, and the skull is the point at which the spectator is involved in what she or he sees. No painting or film can announce directly the spectator's involvement: the attempt to step outside of the fictional space and speak directly to the spectator always fails because the painting or film cannot step outside itself while simultaneously remaining within itself. For instance, any time that a film announces that "this is a film, not reality" we can be sure that it enables the spectator to avoid an encounter with the gaze by telling, rather than by enacting, the spectator's complicity in what she or he sees.[39] But the gaze signals the spectator's involvement indirectly in the form of a distortion in the visual field that shows how the visual field itself takes the spectator's desire into account in its structure.

In *Seminar XI*, where Lacan provides one of his most extended explanations of the gaze, he adds an example from his own life to that of Holbein's *Ambassadors*. He recalls a time in his twenties when he left the safety of his cultured milieu where he grew up and went to work with a group of fishermen in a French coastal town. As he admits, the excitement and danger of this life attracted him to it, but he remained a stranger among the members of the working class with whom he was living. While out at sea one day, one of young fishermen nicknamed Petit-Jean saw a sardine can glistening in the ocean and pointed out to Lacan that though Lacan could see the can, it could not see him. Petit-Jean meant this remark as an insult indicating that Lacan did not belong in the coastal town where he had ensconced himself, that he had no place in the world of the fishing village. But Lacan draws a different lesson from the encounter with the sardine can, a lesson similar to the one that he finds in Holbein's painting.

Though he recounts Petit-Jean's insult, Lacan provides a counterinterpretation of the encounter to the one that Petit-Jean offers. According to Lacan, the sardine can did in fact see Lacan in the sense that it marks Lacan's own distortion of the visual field. He claims, "If what Petit-Jean said to me, namely, that the can did not see me, had any meaning, it was because in a sense, it was looking at me all the same."[40] The sardine can look at Lacan insofar as it distorts the ocean's surface in the same way that Lacan's own perspective and desire distorts life in the fishing village. His desire for the excitement of this life prevents him from having a neutral view of the world he sees there. But this distortion in some form is inescapable. He adds, "I am not simply ... located at the geometral point from which the perspective is grasped. No doubt, in the depths of my eye, the picture is painted. The picture, certainly, is in my eye. But I am in the picture."[41] In addition to the basic biology of seeing—"the picture, certainly, is in my eye"—Lacan notices how desire shapes this act by including the subject within what it sees at the point of the gaze. It is in the distortion of the picture that the subject is included, because the subject's perspective is responsible for distorting what the subject sees. No one can look without the distortion that desire causes.

This understanding of the gaze opens up an approach to the cinema that completely overturns the earlier incarnation of psychoanalytic film theory. Screen theory conceived the gaze in the cinema as a subjective look that creates the illusion of being all-seeing. This illusion has deleterious political effects because it enables the subject to believe itself to exist independently of the visual field that it surveys. This sense of independence corresponds to the individualism that capitalism promulgates and to the interpellation that capitalist ideology enacts. For this reason, Screen theory attacks the gaze as the look of mastery at every point. But to be clear, we should only use the word "look" when referring to Screen theory and confine the word "gaze" to the objet a in the visual field.

The gaze as Lacan theorizes it—located at the stain in the image—is not the site where ideology works on the subject. It is rather the point of a hole within the ideological structure. Cinema's deployment of the gaze determines its ideological valence, but cinema becomes ideological when it obscures the gaze rather than when it highlights it. The turn from Screen theory to a genuine psychoanalytic film theory turns the analysis of film on its head.

Ideology functions by obscuring the subject's involvement in the world that it experiences. It presents the world as fully formed prior to and apart from the subject's desire. This gives the world a solidity that it doesn't really have because the world actually forms around the appeal that it makes to the subject's desire. Without the investment of subjects in it, the world would cease to function, and ideology must work to perpetuate this investment without revealing the dependence of the world on the subjects who constitute it. In the gaze, the subject's role in constituting the world that it sees manifests itself, and the encounter with the gaze in the cinema thus has a radical potential to transform the subject's relationship to its world. This is what recent psychoanalytic film theory uncovers.[42] But most of the time, popular cinema works to hide the gaze and limit cinema's disruptive potential.

# The voice or what is not heard

Though the gaze has historically played the principal role in psychoanalytic discussions of cinema, it is not the only object at play in the filmic experience. The versions of the lost object that Freud conceives are clearly not functioning: even if films may show breasts or feces, no one has tried to turn the film itself into a breast or a mound of excrement, no matter how good or bad the film has been. But this is not the case for the other version of the objet a that Lacan introduces—the voice. Filmmakers have explored the voice as a filmic object, and psychoanalytic film theorists have interpreted the role that the voice plays in cinema.

In one of the initial psychoanalytic interpretations of the voice, Kaja Silverman addresses the voice in the same fashion that Screen theory (specifically Laura Mulvey) addresses the gaze. According to Silverman, symbolic authority resides in the disembodied voice that provides a voiceover and speaks without being seen. This voice is almost exclusively male. The female voice, in contrast, is aligned with a character that the spectator can see, which has the effect of disempowering the woman. In *The Acoustic Mirror*, Silverman writes, "Hollywood's sound regime is another mechanism, analogous to suture, whereby the female subject is obliged to bear a double burden of lack—to absorb the male subject's castration as well as her own."[43] The female character is both seen and heard, while the male character avoids this double ignominy. The voice, like the gaze, is nothing but a vehicle for the marshaling of authority.

Silverman's analysis suffers from the same defect as the Screen theory from which it descends. In the guise of a psychoanalytic approach to cinema, she transforms the desiring subject into a subject of power and thereby erases the essence of psychoanalysis. In the process, she misses how the voice might function as a version of the objet a and not simply as an empirical object that one can easily isolate. Just as the gaze as objet a is not a subject looking, the voice as objet a is not a subject speaking.

The gaze is how the subject's desire distorts the visual field, and, according to Lacan, the voice is how the subject's desire distorts the aural field. The difference between the gaze and voice derives from the difference between the visual and aural fields. The gaze exists at the margin of the image, like the skull at the bottom of Holbein's painting or in the moment when Marion's car ceases to sink in *Psycho*. Due to the nature of the aural field, the voice cannot remain as inconspicuous as the gaze. The moments when the voice distinguishes itself from sound are much rarer in cinema than the moments when the gaze distinguishes itself from the image. Michel Chion identifies the primary form that the voice as objet a assumes.

Chion is the great theorist of the voice in cinema. He invents the concept of the *acousmêtre* in order to account for the voice as a cinematic object. The *acousmêtre* is a voice that appears within the diegetic reality of the film but is attached to no specific representation, like the voice of Mrs Bates in *Psycho* or of Dr Mabuse in *Das Testament des Dr Mabuse* (Fritz Lang 1933).[44] Though Chion doesn't explicitly identify himself with psychoanalytic theory, the *acousmêtre* is a conception of the voice as objet a. When the spectator hears the *acousmêtre*, she or he encounters the voice as a detached object. The voice as objet a manifests the subject's desire because it is what can be heard beyond the regime of sense.

The voice is a disturbance of the aural field. It is the point at which sound ceases to align itself with signification and the partiality or nonneutrality of the aural field becomes apparent. The films that critics traditionally associate with the exploration of cinematic sound, like *The Conversation* (Francis Ford Coppola 1974) or *Blow Out* (Brian DePalma 1981), are usually explorations of the voice as object. This is certainly the case with *The Conversation*, where the repetition of the phrase, "He'd kill us if he had the chance," makes the voice as object apparent.

The film depicts Harry Caul (Gene Hackman), an audio surveillance expert, who is hired to survey a young couple having an affair. In the film's opening sequence, he and his team record the man and woman as they walk through the crowd in San Francisco's Union Square. Through a series of manipulations of the recording, Harry deciphers the man's statement, "He'd kill us if he had the chance." On the basis of this discovery, he assumes that the couple is in danger from the woman's husband, the director (Robert Duvall) of the company that hired Harry. When he first makes out the statement, it seems as if the man stresses the word "kill," which is why Harry believes that the director intends to kill them and that he will be complicit with this murder because he made the recording.

But after the director rather than the couple dies, Harry returns to the recording and hears something quite different. Instead of emphasis on the word "kill," he hears emphasis on the word "us," which indicates that the man was justifying to his paramour the future murder of her husband. By showing how exactly the same statement can completely change its significance based on the desire of the listener, *The Conversation* confronts the spectator with the voice as the point at which desire shapes the aural field. Like Harry, the spectator hears a different statement after knowing about the murder of the director. The encounter with the voice strips away the neutrality of the aural field for the subject.

The voice plays a parallel role to the gaze for psychoanalytic film theory. In both cases, the object intrudes on the spectator's safe distance from the events on the screen and makes evident the spectator's involvement in these events. This means that psychoanalytic theory cannot ignore the voice, but neither should we upbraid film when it focuses its attention on the gaze to the exclusion of the voice. Gaze and voice are two different forms of the same lost object—the object that marks an absence in the visual or aural field and that manifests the subject's desire.

## Antagonism elided

Film relies on the gaze and voice to arouse the spectator's desire. A film without any suggestion of the gaze or voice would be an unwatchable film. There would be nothing to enjoy, no moment that departed from the procession of socially authorized images. But the contrast—a film that produced encounter after encounter with the gaze—is equally unappealing for the spectator. When this occurs, the trauma of the encounter with the real of the gaze becomes normalized and starts to function as a new symbolic construct. The gaze requires the development of a symbolic structure from which it protrudes. Just as Holbein's painting requires the depiction of the two ambassadors and their accumulation of wealth in order for the skull to work as the gaze, a film must establish a diegetic reality in order to reveal the spectator's involvement in it through the gaze. An initial deception about the spectator's position is necessary for the revelation of its truth. Most films, however, do not arrive at the revelation of the truth of the subject. They fail to confront the subject with the gaze in the way that Holbein's painting does. Films distinguish themselves aesthetically and politically on the basis of the relationship that they take up to the gaze.

The primary way that ideology operates in the cinema is not (as Screen theory contends) through identification with the camera or with the characters on the screen but through the depiction and subsequent resolution of the gaze. The resolution of the gaze occurs within a fantasy that accomplishes the impossible. In the course of this ideological operation, the impossible real becomes a symbolic possibility, and the real thus disappears from view. Films that perform this operation have an inherently pacifying effect on spectators. They work to convince the spectator that the trauma of the real is actually nothing but a temporary symbolic hiccup.

We can see this type of ideological resolution of the gaze in the case of *Casablanca* (Michael Curtiz 1942). The film depicts a disruption in the life of Rick Blaine (Humphrey Bogart), an American expatriate running a bar in Morocco during the Second World War. A former love from Rick's past, Ilsa Lund (Ingrid Bergman), comes into Rick's bar one evening with her husband, Victor Laszlo (Paul Henreid). Victor is an opposition leader seeking a Letter of Transit for himself and Ilsa so that they can escape the Nazis, and Rick possesses two letters that would secure their freedom. The film revolves around two competing ideological fantasies centering on Rick—on the one hand, a reunion with Ilsa, and on the other, heroically assisting Victor in his escape.

The coexistence of two competing and irreconcilable ideological imperatives indicates that the film touches on the real. It reveals the antagonistic nature of the symbolic order to the spectator. One sees how the symbolic demands contradict each other and lead to an avoidable impasse. This impasse is the real, and it is the point at which the spectator's desire engages the film. During most of the running time of *Casablanca*, the gaze is lurking in the form of the impasse between the competing ideological imperatives, but the film's conclusion domesticates the gaze and enables the spectator to have enjoyed it without confronting the inherent trauma of this enjoyment. But the ending of *Casablanca* is not as politically disastrous as it might have been.

*Casablanca* rejects the cheap resolution that would have Ilsa stay behind with Rick while they aid Victor in escaping alone. This type of resolution is common in popular cinema. The conclusion of *The Dark Knight Rises* (Christopher Nolan 2012), for instance, depicts Batman (Christian Bale) confronted with impasse of two competing imperatives—a romantic union with Selina Kyle (Anne Hathaway) and saving the city of Gotham by sacrificing his life. Rather than choosing, Batman is able miraculously to accomplish both: he apparently dies saving the city as he flies an atomic bomb over the ocean to explode, but then he ends up in a café in Europe with Selina during the film's epilogue. Through this typical ending, *The Dark Knight Rises* resolves the antagonism that animates the film and reveals to the spectator that, in fact, the antagonism was not an antagonism at all but just a surmountable difficulty. This is also the effect of the conclusion of *Casablanca*, but *Casablanca* accomplishes the resolution of the antagonism with more fantasmatic dexterity.

If *Casablanca* were *The Dark Knight Rises*, Ilsa would stay behind with Rick while Victor flew away to safety. Curtiz opts for a different path to the same ideological effect. Ilsa leaves with Victor, but before she leaves, she reveals that she loves Rick rather than Victor. Rick decides that she must leave not because duty to the resistance is more important than their love (which is what he tells her) but because their love is so powerful that physical separation will not interfere with it. The ending of *Casablanca* diminishes neither the imperative of the romantic union nor that of heroism, but it allows the two antagonistic imperatives to coexist. Though the real antagonism drives the narrative of the film, it drops out in the end and allows the spectator to accept that the symbolic structure works effectively. This final turn marks the disappearance of the gaze from the film.

The gaze is real, and the antagonistic nature of the symbolic order must be evident for the gaze to appear. When a film resolves its structuring antagonism, the gaze recedes, and an image of completeness replaces it. At this point, the symbolic reality of the film becomes self-contained, and the spectator's involvement in the structuring of that reality becomes invisible. The encounter with the gaze in the cinema depends on the presence of antagonism. When the antagonism disappears in *Casablanca* and *The Dark Knight Rises*, these films hide the gaze. This action of relying on the gaze and then hiding it is the chief ideological operation of cinema.

Ideology proclaims that antagonism does not exist and that there is nothing necessary about trauma. This frees the subject to believe that the symbolic order operates smoothly on its own without the involvement of the subject itself. Ideology gives the subject the illusion of a neutral and enduring background that guarantees the significance of the subject's actions. Film plays an ideological role in society when it contributes to the subject's belief and investment in this illusory neutral background. This is what happens with most films. But the possibility exists for films to turn against their ideological function and to create an encounter with the gaze that alerts the spectator to the trauma of the real antagonism rather than obscuring it.

# Antagonism exposed

Though cinema most often operates in the manner of *Casablanca* and allows the spectator to avoid confronting the implications of the encounter with the gaze (and thus confronting the social antagonism), film is an important artistic medium because there are films that thwart this avoidance and instead facilitate an encounter with the gaze. No film avoids the gaze altogether, but most do their best to minimize its trauma. But nonetheless, every trip to the cinema or every time we sit down to watch a film at home presents us with the possibility for the encounter with the gaze. Though it is inherently traumatic, the gaze drives our spectatorship. If there were no possibility for the encounter with the gaze, no one would watch a film. In the gaze, we see the truth of our desire.

*M* (1931) is Fritz Lang's masterpiece because it refuses to resolve the antagonism in the way that *Casablanca* does.[45] The film recounts a series of child murders that take place in Berlin during the Weimar Republic. Lang divides the spectator's attention between those pursuing the murderer and the murderer himself, Hans Beckert (Peter Lorre). This split in the spectator's attention establishes the film's fundamental antagonism. The spectator's desire inevitably aligns with the children and the public trying to protect them. But at the same time, Beckert is the one character individualized in the film's narrative, and this forces the spectator's desire to his side, despite his horrific actions.

Lang doesn't shy away from the horror of the murder of a child in order to create sympathy for Beckert. In fact, he structures the film as he does in order to focus on the trauma of the child murders. *M* doesn't portray Beckert as a sympathetic figure, but it also doesn't allow the spectator to have an uncomplicated desire in relation to him. This complication reaches its high point in the film's most important scene. After members of the public pursue Beckert, they lead him to a kangaroo court in an old warehouse.

The key scene in *Casablanca* occurs at the airport, when Rick heroically allows Ilsa to leave and proclaim that their love transcends physical distance. This resolution of the film's fundamental antagonism spares the spectator from the gaze. The key scene in *M* moves in the opposite direction. It is the kangaroo court scene, in which the Berlin underworld conspires with other citizens to enact its own form of justice on Beckert. Lang films this scene in a way that highlights the antagonism of the film rather than obscuring it, but even the decision to include the kangaroo court scene indicates the film's commitment to highlighting the contradictions of the symbolic system rather than eliding them.

By showing the criminals' kangaroo court preceding the depiction of the actual trial, Lang reveals that the criminals have a status internal to the law, unlike the child murderer Beckert. Though the criminals violate the written laws of Berlin society, they continue to belong to Berlin society. Their disobedience doesn't extend to the society's unwritten rules. Beckert, in contrast, must endure complete exclusion from the social order. His acts of child murder violate both the written laws and the unwritten rules, and he is thus far worse off than the criminals. In relation to him, they are insiders and can sit in judgment on him.

In the scene where they do sit in judgment, Lang constructs it so as to emphasize the spectator's alignment with the horrific child murderer. The scene depicts a threatening mass of people full of hatred, and it contrasts this mass with the isolated Beckert. Lang films Beckert articulating his defense by isolating him in the shot, after several shots of the angry mob. The juxtaposition of the threatening crowd and the isolated child murderer has the effect of forcing the spectator's desire into an alignment with that of the child murderer. At this moment in the film, the spectator encounters the gaze and, through the gaze, the fundamental antagonism of the social order.

While watching *M*, the spectator recognizes that modern society cannot reconcile the claims of the individual with those of justice, and this failure highlights the insubstantiality of the symbolic order. This order contradicts itself. As a result, it relies on the investment of the subject's desire for its sustenance. When we see our desire manifested on the screen, we simultaneously see, as Žižek is fond of repeating, that the big Other does not exist. The symbolic structure relies on the subject's investment because it cannot rely on itself, and the task of cinema consists in paying attention to this inability.

The zenith of cinematic art occurs with the encounter with the gaze and the voice. Screen theory was undoubtedly correct to make the act of looking a central axis of its approach to cinema, but this theory never sees what it's looking for. The gaze is the disruption of the look and the site of cinema's potential radicality. The political danger is not that cinema employs the gaze but that it elides it. Psychoanalytic film theory takes the gaze and voice as its points of departure not because these objects form the last word on cinema but because they are the points at which enjoyment manifests itself in the cinematic form. The key to a psychoanalytic approach to film lies in theorizing how films formally address the spectator's desire and enjoyment, how they construct fantasies that appeal to the spectator's desire and that enable the spectator to enjoy through the confrontation with a real antagonism.

# Notes

1   Throughout this discussion of Freud and Lacan, I will not address the various stages of development of their theories. Though there were clearly different moments in their theoretical elaboration that sometimes involved dramatic changes in course, this book will focus on the essential contribution that each theorist makes to psychoanalytic theory, and it will present psychoanalytic theory as a total system for interpretation. Obviously, this decision involves an elision of not only history but also what doesn't fit within this essential kernel. (For instance, there will be no discussion at all of Freud's concept of the id or Lacan's concept of the four discourses). This elision

creates a coherency that doesn't exist, but I hope that it also captures the unique contribution that psychoanalysis has to make to the interpretation of culture in general and film in specific.

2   Freud first announces this tripartite schema in *The Interpretation of Dreams* (1900), and he labels it the topographic theory. Later, when he writes *The Ego and the Id* (1923), he supplements the topographic theory with a structural one, which divides the psyche into id, ego, and superego. Though Freud doesn't design the structural theory as a replacement for the topographic theory, it does become much more well known because it allows adherents to gravitate toward the ego as a stable and controlling center for the psyche. To the extent that the structural theory makes this move possible, we should lament its introduction, though perhaps the fecund concept of the superego makes up for the deleterious effect of the concept of the ego.

3   Hartmann's goal for psychoanalysis is the elimination of the unconscious disturbance in the psychic life of the subject. He writes, "Generally speaking, we call a man well adapted if his productivity, his ability to enjoy life, and his mental equilibrium are undisturbed." Heniz Hartmann, *Ego Psychology and the Problem of Adaptation*, trans. David Rapaport (Madison: International Universities Press, 1958), 23.

4   According to Freud, "If someone talks of subconsciousness, I cannot tell whether he means the term topographically—to indicate something lying in the mind beneath consciousness—or qualitatively—to indicate another consciousness, a subterranean one, as it were. He is probably not clear about any of it. The only trustworthy antithesis is between conscious and unconscious." Sigmund Freud, *The Question of Lay Analysis*, trans. James Strachey, in *The Complete Psychological Works of Sigmund Freud*, vol. 20, ed. James Strachey (London: Hogarth, 1959), 198.

5   The fact that the unconscious is a surface phenomenon shows how incorrect it is to label Freud a "deep psychologist." Both terms are wrong. He is not a psychologist at all because the psyche that he analyzes is not an internal mind that has a substantial existence but a surface that is always expressing itself.

6   Those who see Freud as an unavowed follower (or even plagiarist) of Friedrich Nietzsche make the mistake of conflating power with desire. Though Freud clearly admired Nietzsche as a thinker, the philosophical distance between them is immense.

7   Despite Freud's appreciation for Darwin and his belief that he followed in Darwin's lineage, the clear distinction between their positions has become fully evident today. The Neo-Darwinist explanation of behavior reduces the desiring subject to a self-interested being, whereas psychoanalysis contends that the subject is no longer capable of acting in its own interest, except as a path toward its eventual subversion.

8   See Immanuel Kant, *The Critique of Pure Reason*, trans. Paul Guyer and Allen W. Wood (Cambridge: Cambridge University Press, 1998).

9   Jacques Lacan, "The Signification of the Phallus," in *Écrits: The First Complete Edition in English*, trans. Bruce Fink (New York: Norton, 2006), 580.

10   This statement occurs in Lacan's first seminar, and he repeats it on several occasions in later seminars. Despite its fundamental importance for understanding his thought, it appears nowhere in his *Écrits* (the collected writings). This goes to show that the path toward understanding Lacan's thought runs through his oral seminars rather than through any of his written work.

11   It is easy to confuse the signified with the referent, the object to which the signifier refers, but this distinction is important. The signified is the meaning or mental image that accompanies the signifier, not the object in reality that it references.

12   The philosophical focus on the will at the expense of the signifier represents an attempt to give consciousness an authority over the unconscious. This is clearly evident in the case of Arthur Schopenhauer. Following what he imagines to be Kant's position, Schopenhauer divides existence into the world of representation (or the signifier) and that of the will. Though we believe in the priority of representations, Schopenhauer insists that it is will that actually determines these representations. Will, for Schopenhauer, is the Kantian thing in itself. Though Schopenhauer does refer to the will as unconscious, he means by this only that the will is not

conscious. He himself has no difficulty bringing the will to consciousness.

**13** One could argue that the fundamental antagonism for psychoanalysis is sexual difference, but this is just a translation of the antagonism between the individual and the social order. Female subjectivity resides on the side of the individual, and male subjectivity on the side of the social order.

**14** Sigmund Freud, *Civilization and Its Discontents*, trans. James Strachey, in *The Standard Edition of the Complete Psychological Works of Sigmund Freud*, vol. 22, ed. James Strachey (London: Hogarth Press, 1961), 86.

**15** Jung's anti-Semitism is not just an anomaly of his particular individuality but has theoretical roots. One who believes in opposition rather than antagonism is more given to anti-Semitism since the Jew represents the intruder that disrupts the balance of the opposing forces. For one who believes in the irreducibility of antagonism, anti-Semitism is an impossible position to adopt.

**16** The objet a makes its first appearance in Lacan's thought in *Seminar X* where he discusses anxiety, though Lacan hints at it in *Seminar VIII* on the transference when he describes what makes Socrates desirable to Alcibiades in Plato's *Symposium*. See Jacques Lacan, *The Seminar of Jacques Lacan, Book X: Anxiety*, ed. Jacques-Alain Miller, trans. A. R. Price (Malden, MA: Polity, 2014).

**17** Jacques Lacan, *Le Séminaire XXI: Les non-dupes errant*, unpublished manuscript, session of April 9, 1974.

**18** There are many Lacanian theorists who reject the translation of jouissance and believe that the English word "enjoyment" fails to communicate both the extremity and the complexity of the French word. This is why Bruce Fink, for instance, leaves "jouissance" untranslated in his translation of Lacan's *Écrits*. The problem with this insistence on the impossibility of translating "jouissance" is that it indulges in precisely the fantasy of a lost substantial origin that psychoanalysis attacks at every instance. Thus, I will move freely between the two terms—"jouissance" and "enjoyment"—without distinguishing between them.

19   Jacques Lacan, "The Subversion of the Subject and the Dialectic of Desire in the Freudian Unconscious," in *Écrits: The First Complete Edition in English*, trans. Bruce Fink (New York: Norton, 2006), 694.

20   See Jacques Lacan, "The Mirror Stage as Formative of the *I* Function," in *Écrits: The First Complete Edition in English*, trans. Bruce Fink (New York: Norton, 2006), 75–81.

21   See Jacques-Alain Miller, "Suture (Notes on the Logic of the Signifier)," trans. Jacqueline Rose, *Screen* 18.4 (1978): 24–34.

22   Lacan makes just this point in his seminar on the object of psychoanalysis. He states, "The objet a is what we can never grasp and especially not in the mirror." Jacques Lacan, *Le Séminaire XIII: L'objet de la psychanalyse*, unpublished manuscript, session of May 18, 1966.

23   Laura Mulvey, "Visual Pleasure and Narrative Cinema," in *Movies and Methods*, vol. 2, ed. Bill Nichols (Berkeley: University of California Press, 1985), 309.

24   See Jean-Pierre Oudart, "Suture and Cinema," trans. Kari Hanet, *Screen* 18.4 (1978): 35–47.

25   Daniel Dayan, "The Tutor-Code of Classical Cinema," *Film Quarterly* 28.1 (1974): 31. In this essay, Dayan includes multiple misleading and even baldly inaccurate statements about Lacan's version of psychoanalysis. For instance, he claims that Lacan calls psychoanalysis a science and that he views psychoanalysis as a theory of intersubjectivity. Most egregious of all, Dayan claims that Lacan had recourse to the concept of the imaginary in order to avoid the tired concept of subjectivity, which he rejected thoroughly. Dayan's summary of Lacan today reads like a caricature, but to be fair, printed versions of the seminars were not as readily available in the early 1970s as they are today, and interpreting Lacan solely on the basis of his *Écrits* is certainly a vexed, if not impossible, enterprise.

26   Rose points out that the reality effect that Screen theory criticizes is a reality effect that its conception of the cinema creates. In her discussion of Christian Metz, she notes, "By confining the concept of the imaginary within the debate about realism, Metz made the spectator's position in the cinema (the fantasy of the all-perceiving subject) a mirror image of the

error underpinning an idealist ontology of film (cinema as a ceaseless and gradually perfected appropriation of reality)." Jacqueline Rose, *Sexuality in the Field of Vision* (London: Verso, 1986), 201.

27  Though Copjec acknowledges Rose's importance at two points in her essay, she also notes this absence of absence—or absence of the real—in Rose's critique of Screen theory.

28  Joan Copjec, "The Orthopsychic Subject," *October* 49 (1989): 69–70.

29  I appreciate Joan Copjec's generous assistance in supplying me with the original documents from this conference, including Bellour's response to her essay.

30  Raymond Bellour, "Cher amis de *Hors Cadre*...," *Hors Cadre* 7 (1989): 52.

31  Bellour, "Cher amis de *Hors Cadre*...," 52.

32  David Bordwell, "Contemporary Film Studies and the Vicissitudes of Grand Theory," in *Post-Theory: Reconstructing Film Studies* (Madison: University of Wisconsin Press, 1996), 24.

33  The one time where Žižek does address Screen theory occurs in the only book that he devotes entirely to film theory, but the primary object of this work is not Screen theory but an attempt to reclaim the importance of psychoanalytic theory for film studies after the attack launched by David Bordwell and Noël Carroll in *Post-Theory*. For this discussion, see Slavoj Žižek, *The Fright of Real Tears: Krzysztof Kieslowski Between Theory and Post-Theory* (London: British Film Institute, 2001).

34  Slavoj Žižek, *The Sublime Object of Ideology* (London: Verso, 1989), 47.

35  Stephen Heath, "Cinema and Psychoanalysis: Parallel Histories," in *Endless Night: Cinema and Psychoanalysis, Parallel Histories*, ed. Janet Bergstrom (Berkeley: University of California Press, 1999), 44.

36  Vicky Lebeau, *Psychoanalysis and Cinema: The Play of Shadows* (London: Wallflower Press, 2001), 59.

37  The film theorists that Žižek has influenced are numerous and include Jennifer Friedlander, Sheila Kunkle, Hugh Manon, Hilary Neroni, and Fabio Vighi. For a sampling of Žižek's

influence on film and media theory, see Matthew Flisfeder and Louis-Paul Willis (eds), *Žižek and Media Studies Reader* (New York: Palgrave, 2014).

38 Lacan, *Le Séminaire XIII: L'objet de la psychanalyse*, session of May 18, 1966.

39 The tedium of Jean-Luc Godard's late films stems directly from his attempt to announce the spectator's involvement in what she or he sees. Though Godard's early films like *Vivre sa vie* (1962) and *Le Mépris* (*Contempt*, 1963) deploy the gaze in order to trap the spectator's desire, his later films such as *King Lear* (1987) and *Film socialisme* (2010) emphasize at every turn that they are constructed for the spectator. This appeal to the spectator's consciousness deflects the possibility of exposing the spectator's unconscious investment in the images on the screen.

40 Jacques Lacan, *The Seminar of Jacques Lacan, Book XI: The Four Fundamental Concepts of Psychoanalysis*, ed. Jacques-Alain Miller, trans. Alan Sheridan (New York: Norton, 1978), 95.

41 Lacan, *Seminar XI*, 96 (translation corrected). Sheridan's translation of *Seminar XI* manages to communicate the exact opposite of what Lacan says in French. The last line of the paragraph in French reads, "Mais moi je suis dans le tableau." Sheridan translates this as: "But I am not in the picture." The miraculous appearance of the "not" completely transforms the sense and obscures the central point in Lacan's discussion of the gaze. Anyone relying on this translation would simply be cast adrift at this moment.

42 For a more complete elaboration of this argument, see Todd McGowan, *The Real Gaze: Film Theory After Lacan* (Albany: SUNY Press, 2007).

43 Kaja Silverman, *The Acoustic Mirror: The Female Voice in Psychoanalysis and Cinema* (Bloomington: Indiana University Press, 1988), 63.

44 For Chion's discussion of the *acousmêtre*, see Michel Chion, *The Voice in Cinema*, trans. Claudia Gorbman (New York: Columbia University Press, 1999).

45 *M* represents one of the rare cases where a filmmaker correctly grasps the value of her or his own work. Lang himself always considered it his greatest film, despite the many outstanding possibilities that both preceded and followed it.

# CHAPTER TWO

# Psychoanalysis and *The Rules of the Game*

## Speaking to the unconscious

Jean Renoir's *La Regle du jeu* (*The Rules of the Game*, 1939) marks the conclusion of the most creative period in his filmmaking career. It serves as an exclamation point that gives this moment in his career its shape. This period begins with *Le Crime de Monsieur Lange* (1936) and continues through *Les Bas-fonds* (*The Lower Depths*, 1936), *Une Partie de campagne* (*A Day in the Country*, 1936), *La Grande Illusion* (1937), *La Marseillaise* (1937), and *La Bête humaine* (*The Human Beast*, 1938). Though Renoir had what many critics consider great achievements like *Boudu sauvé des eaux* (*Boudu Saved from Drowning* (1932) and *The River* (1951) before and after this period, the burst of creativity that occurred during the late 1930s had no equal during the rest of his filmmaking career.[1] His earlier films lacked the filmic scope and complexity, and his later films lacked the intense social critique and political awareness that marked the films of this period.

The films from this period are commonly known as Renoir's Popular Front films. In response to Hitler's rise to power in Germany and Mussolini's in Italy along with the burgeoning of fascist groups in France, Renoir committed himself to the antifascist Left and became a fellow traveler of the communist party, though he never joined the party. *Le Crime de Monsieur Lange* marks the beginning of Renoir's engaged cinema, and most critics believe that *The Rules of the Game* leaves this period behind. As will become clear, my argument is that *The Rules of the Game* is Renoir's most significant political film. Its political commitment is less direct than that of an overtly communist film like his 1936 *La Vie est à nous* (*Life Belongs to Us*), but the political power of *The Rules of the Game* stems from its thoroughgoing critique of the abandonment of engaged politics for the security of cynical distance.[2] Its political intervention is not straightforwardly evident but occurs on different levels—from shot composition and editing to dialogue and performance—and this is what necessitates a psychoanalytic approach in order to uncover it.

When deciding on Renoir's masterpiece, there are really only two serious options—*La Grande Illusion* or *The Rules of the Game*. Orson Welles nicely embodies the dilemma, at times expressing his belief that the former would be the film that he would take with him to a desert island and on other occasions claiming that the latter was the greatest film ever made. But most film historians and scholars have now come to a consensus and see *The Rules of the Game* as the achievement that Renoir had been building toward. For example, William Rothman argues that "*The Rules of the Game* brings a series of films, Renoir's lifework up to that time, to completion. It is not that a certain project is arbitrarily broken off, but that *The Rules of the Game* constitutes the fulfillment of Renoir's original filmmaking project."[3] *The Rules of the Game* fully develops the aesthetic and political concerns present in *La Grande Illusion*.

One measure of the film's importance lies in the hostility that greeted it on its release. Of course, not every film that earns public and critical disapprobation is a masterpiece—most are just failures—but the film that challenges the ideological structures and fantasmatic investments of its time almost inevitably receives some measure of disdain. Films that simply fail usually provoke indifference rather than open hostility.

This hostility is the measure of the traumatic interruption that the film delivers to the psyche of spectators at the time of its release.

Later, one integrates the formerly traumatic film into the canon of cinematic masterpieces and thereby diffuses the trauma of its emergence. One can appreciate such masterpieces from a distance, just as one regards museum pieces. Giving a film the status of the cinematic masterpiece is an attempt at once to acknowledge and eliminate its importance as a challenge to the existing social order and to the psyche of the subjects of that order. The very appreciation that a masterpiece engenders is inimical to the experience of the masterpiece's traumatic weight. But if *The Rules of the Game* represents the zenith of Renoir's cinema, it nonetheless unleashes its critique on the spectator indirectly.

The great film cannot simply announce its greatness and unleash an unrelenting critique on the spectator. Such a film would have no spectators. It must instead set a trap for the unconscious of the spectator. This is what Jean Renoir's *The Rules of the Game* accomplishes, and what gives this film its lasting significance. The fact that it shares with *Citizen Kane* (Orson Welles 1941) a tortured postproduction history is not coincidental. Threatened by William Randolph Hurst, fellow studio executives offered RKO pictures almost a million dollars to destroy the negative of Welles's film, and Renoir had to modify *The Rules of the Game* in order to appease resistant critics and audiences. Neither Renoir's original version or the premiere version survives, and at one point, the general neglect of the film (along with allied bombs) led to the fear that the film was lost. The danger that films such as *Citizen Kane* and *The Rules of the Game* pose lies precisely in their appeal to the unconscious. Renoir makes spectators aware of their unconscious investment in obedience, which is an investment that the social order prefers to keep hidden.[4] Social authority depends on hiding the psychic investment in authority of those under its rule. As a result, the demise of *The Rules of the Game* after its release should not be surprising. Given its indictment of the spectators' investment in the authority that subjects them, it is instead stunning that audiences ever came to appreciate the film.[5]

Though critics and audiences implicitly recognized the danger that Renoir's film presented and rejected it, the film does manage to appeal to spectators by allowing them to find enjoyment in the exposure of their pathological investment in obedience. The great achievement of the film is that it allows the spectator to enjoy witnessing a critique that frees her or him from the psychic investments that are most enthralling. The simple act of watching *The Rules of the Game* is an act of freeing oneself from the debilitating unconscious investment in obedience.

But Renoir understands that spectators don't go to films in order to discover the truth of their unconscious investments. Even the spectators of documentary films don't have such pure motives. Instead, one watches a film because the film promises enjoyment, and *The Rules of the Game* locates the spectator's enjoyment in the discovery of this disturbing unconscious investment in authority. The revelations of the film both disturb and delight, and Renoir reveals that the power of an aesthetic work to expose the unconscious is integral to its formal structure and the enjoyment that this structure provides. The wager of Renoir's masterpiece is that one can enjoy watching oneself be undone, and this is what occurs when the film exhibits the excessive obedience that always threatens our subjectivity and that threatened the entire world at the exact time of the film's release.[6]

It is easy to understand why individuals obey the dictates of their society and why every society requires this obedience. If certain individuals could disobey with impunity, then everyone else would refuse to accept the social pact, and it would crumble. In this way, obedience makes sense. No one needs psychoanalysis to explain obedience, and yet psychoanalysis as such emerges out of the struggles that subjects have with their obedience to the social law. In the psyche of the subject, the law doesn't simply remain an external force but prompts a psychic investment on the subject's part. The law distorts the psyche of those subjected to it, and this distortion is never plainly visible. It necessitates psychoanalysis to expose the psychic implications of subjection to the law. We cannot simply obey an external law, and it is this fact that led to the birth of psychoanalysis. The law seduces the subject into a psychic investment in it through its own internal division, its inconsistency.[7]

The problem is that it is impossible to obey the law from a distance, to obey without developing a psychic attachment to the law and the authority that supports it. This attachment becomes the source of our obedience and the barrier to any freedom from the dictates of social authority. Obviously, there are authoritarian regimes that rule through force, but even these regimes depend on a psychic investment of those subjected in order to continue functioning. Even a fascist government cannot rule by brute force alone. It requires the psychic commitment of those who have no good reason to commit themselves. This investment is the sine qua non of social existence, and it marks the fundamental barrier to social change.

The radicality of *The Rules of the Game* lies in its confrontation with our excessive obedience and in its attempt to render this obedience untenable. It is as if the film is itself a member of the French Resistance prior to the existence of this entity. Renoir's film doesn't challenge the ruling social authority head on in the way that a resistance movement would, but it does undermine the psychic benefits accruing from obedience.[8] *The Rules of the Game* demands spectators who recognize their own complicity in what constrains them and must therefore reject it. No fascist sympathizer can be said to have genuinely seen *The Rules of the Game*.

## The real *Rules of the Game*

The traumatic disruption that *The Rules of the Game* delivers is not only evident in the film's content and formal structure; it also manifests itself directly in the popular and critical reception. Though some critics expressed appreciation, the general critical reception was as negative as the public reception. The negative initial response to the film was overwhelming and reflects the power that it had to disrupt the assumptions of the social order at the time. The discrepancy between the initial popular and critical reception and the current critical consensus is probably greater in the case of *The Rules of the Game* than with any other film in the history of cinema.

Even before the film's release, Renoir had to censor his own film to make it more acceptable for a popular audience. His initial preview version was, according to Renoir himself and other accounts, 113 minutes, but the version that premiered was much shorter. Renoir acquiesced to concerns from the film's financial backers and exhibitors when he cut the preview version. The 94-minute version premiered at an upscale Parisian theater, La Colisée, on July 7, 1939.[9] The response was overwhelmingly, but not uniformly, negative. Booing and hissing occurred during the film, and a man purportedly set a newspaper on fire at the theater in order to express his distaste for the film.[10]

The hostility made an impression on everyone who attended the screening, and it spread beyond the original screening. According to V. F. Perkins,

> There is little room for doubt that *La Règle du jeu* was widely scorned and hated. Too many people who were there at the time—among others, the actors Marcel Dalio and Paulette Dubost, the set designer Eugène Lourié and Henri Cartier-Bresson, an assistant director on the film— left testimony that supports Renoir's memory of a painful rejection. In its wake, further cuts were made as the director attempted to get rid of incidents that seemed particularly to rile the spectators, only to find that hostility erupted elsewhere in what remained.[11]

From the 94-minute truncated version, Renoir quickly re-worked the film and released a new expurgated version that was 81 minutes long and, he believed, less offensive to the public.

The creation of a shortened version of the film was an act of repression. Though Renoir acted consciously (which would seem to rule out repression because one cannot consciously repress), he responded to the unconscious exigencies of the public. This act of repression testifies to the traumatic status of the film even more than the eyewitness reports from the July 7 premiere. We can interpret trauma through repression rather than vice versa. When we see an act of repression, we know that an encounter with the real has taken place.

The fact that Renoir's act of repression did not make the film more acceptable to audiences provides an insight into repression. Though it removes traumatic ideas (or scenes in this case), repression never works. The traumatic effect remains when the idea is hidden from consciousness because the trauma stems from a gap in significance—an encounter with a lack of sense—and repression leaves the gap in place even as it eliminates the idea. This is why, as Freud insists, repression always makes the trauma worse for the subject (and why there is no psychic danger associated with lifting repression). Repression increases the failure of sense rather than ameliorating it.

Renoir's 81-minute version of *The Rules of the Game* met with as much popular disdain as the 94-minute version. But the ultimate act of censorship occurred during the war, when the negative and most extant copies of the film disappeared, either through willful acts of destruction or through the vagaries of war. It seemed as if the original version of *The Rules of the Game* was bound to have the status of a lost classic, akin to Orson Welles' original version of *The Magnificent Ambersons* (1942). It is the case, in fact, that the 94-minute premiere version of the film no longer exists, and no one can precisely reconstruct it. But what we have now is better than the original.[12]

A group of film enthusiasts in Paris formed La Société des Grands Films Classiques, and this organization acquired all the negative and positive pieces of *The Rules of the Game* that they could find. A great discovery of material made possible an unprecedented act of filmic reconstruction. As Perkins describes,

Buoyed by their discovery of salvaged material in another laboratory—more than two hundred cans of it—Jean Gaborit and Jacques Maréchal worked with the editor Jacques Durand to reconstitute Renoir's movie. They went beyond restoration of the first premiere version to achieve something close to the 113 minutes that Renoir had initially sanctioned. Although the term did not exist in 1959, their edition of *La Règle du jeu* was surely the first and still the most glorious instance in cinema history of a Director's Cut.[13]

Gaborit and Maréchal created a 106-minute version of the film that has become the accepted version of the film. Though Renoir did not play a role in this reconstruction, he did accept it as the authorized version of the film. But even if it lacked his approval, a comparison of the edited version and the reconstruction reveals the latter's superiority.[14] The reconstruction also makes clear why the film had a traumatic impact on the audiences and critics of the time, an impact that Renoir himself anticipated when he cut his initial preview version of the film.

The reconstruction of the authentic version of *The Rules of the Game* twenty years after its release evinces a process that Freud calls *Nachträglichkeit* or retroactivity. According to Freud, the subject cannot recognize a trauma at the instant it occurs. It is only after the fact or retroactively that the subject recognizes how the traumatic event shaped its psyche, and at this later moment, the subject, as it were, experiences the trauma for the first time through its repetition. Or to put it in the terms of Lacan (for whom *Nachträglichkeit* played an even more expansive role in his thought than that of Freud), the traumatic real has the status of the real only when the subject recognizes the network of signification that this real disrupts.

The real *Rules of the Game* exists only retroactively. The original version constitutes a traumatic absence that the reconstructed version establishes after the fact. One shouldn't go so far as to say that if someone discovers Renoir's preview version of the film, she or he should destroy it (as Claude Lanzmann famously said about the possibility of discovering documentary footage from Auschwitz). But the reconstruction captures the trauma of the original and thus renders its discovery unnecessary.

The existence of the reconstruction of *The Rules of the Game* provides spectators with the opportunity to see exactly what constituted the trauma of its reception. Even though the film is 12 minutes longer than the version that the original audience saw and experienced as a trauma, the inclusion of material that Renoir himself censored before the premiere does not obfuscate our understanding of the nature of the trauma. When we look at the reconstruction and its additional material—including a crucial scene near the end where the film forces an encounter with the gaze—we are seeing the real *Rules of the Game*.

# An excess of genre

One of the predominant ways that the symbolic order functions in cinema is through the mediation of genre. Genres are symbolic categories that govern our expectations when we watch a film. Generic labels tell us what films to avoid (like westerns) and what films to see (like romantic comedies). Locating a film within a genre lessens the trauma of encountering it for the audience. If we know, for instance, that we're going to a horror film, this mitigates the trauma of seeing someone's head cut off or a dead person coming back to life. Generic codes help to keep the encounter with the traumatic real at bay while watching a film.

But accessing the real is not as simple as dispensing with genre altogether. There are many films that don't fit within any generic category, and audiences watch them without any difficulty at all. The spectator of *The King's Speech* (Tom Hooper 2010) would probably have difficulty placing it within a genre (other than the nondescript "drama" category), but this doesn't provide the film with any traumatic impact. In fact, the point of the film lies in erasing a potential traumatic encounter for the spectator rather than facilitating one. Abandoning genre is not abandoning the symbolic for the real, and one always operates within some type of generic categories, even when these categories are only implicit.

We should thus not be too quick to laud the difficulties of classifying *The Rules of the Game* in a particular genre. Many films avoid genre in order to obfuscate their direct adherence to the symbolic demands that govern filmmaking. But the difference between *The King's Speech* and *The Rules of the Game* in relation to genre is significant. Whereas the former merely evades genre, the latter deliberately confounds it. There is a difference, in other words, between a film that doesn't occupy a generic category and one that attempts to disturb the expectations of spectators by promising one genre and then delivering another. *The Rules of the Game* doesn't just present itself as a comedy and then confront the spectator with horror; instead, it constantly moves between genres so that the spectator cannot find a comfortable position from which to view the film. This movement from genre to genre is integral to the traumatic power that the film has.

This is the contention of James Leahy. According to Leahy,

> *La Règle du jeu* is all the more disturbing because so many of the characters are so likeable, their repeated inability to make a correct or decisive choice (echoing the political indecisiveness of the nation itself) resulting from generosity and understanding. Not surprisingly, audiences found the film's vision, and its changes of pace and tone, from drawing-room comedy through farce to tragedy and cover-up, intolerable.[15]

While watching *The Rules of the Game*, one can find oneself laughing at one moment, horrified at the next, and then laughing again soon thereafter. This is not inconsistency on Renoir's part but a commitment to showing a prevailing attitude in which nothing disturbs the characters. What is truly disturbing about *The Rules of the Game* is the lack of disturbance that we see in the film.

From the beginning, the film seems as if it will be a piece of undemanding entertainment. Renoir's title card labels the film a "fantasie dramatique" (dramatic fantasy), but the epigram from Beaumarchais' *Le Mariage de Figaro* (*The Marriage of Figaro*) suggests less drama and more comedy as it promises lightheartedness. But this lightheartedness disappears right away with the arrival of André Jurieux (Roland Toutain) in Paris after a transatlantic flight. There is a mob of people surrounding André, but there is nothing comic about the scene. André is fatigued and depressed that the woman he has flown to see isn't there to greet him after his great achievement.

The rest of the film follows from the type of contrast that Renoir establishes between the title card and the first scene. The tone shifts in an instant throughout the running time. At no point does the film rest stably within a particular genre, but it never abandons genre altogether. It uses genre to establish the spectator's expectations and then quickly confound them.

*The Rules of the Game* often turns from comedy to serious traumatic drama. This occurs most famously during the hunting sequence, where the slaughter of many animals follows the idle and jocular banter of the characters. The slaughter has much more traumatic impact than it otherwise would due to the situation that precedes it. And later, André becomes a murder victim after the characters perform a farcical masquerade and after comic gunplay within the estate results in no injuries at all. Guns seem like harmless comic props that create what one character labels a "comédie" until a gun results in André's death. Seriousness is always ready to erupt traumatically out of comedy in the film.

But the real trauma in the film lies in the opposite turn—when seriousness becomes comedy. The characters in the film evince a profound ability to retreat back into their comic roles after the most traumatic events, including the death of André at the end of the film. The traumatic impact of *The Rules of the Game* on the spectator lies in the absence of any impact of the traumatic events on the characters. This switch in genre—from traumatic drama back to comedy—is the most disturbing one that Renoir employs, and he does so in order to indict the cynicism that the characters evince. This cynicism pervades all the classes depicted in the film, and the criticism of it separates *The Rules of the Game* from Renoir's earlier films.


# From class to nation

It is tempting to interpret *The Rules of the Game* as a film, like *La Grande Illusion*, about class division. The earlier film makes a clear political claim by showing how class division trumps national identity. Though the film is not explicitly Marxist in orientation, its controlling idea lies in the vein of Marxism: class antagonism, not war between nation-states, is the fundamental antagonism of modernity.[16] In *La Grande Illusion*, members of the aristocracy feel more at home with each other even when they are on opposing sides in war than do compatriots of different classes. The memorable final scene of this film, which depicts French prisoners fleeing Germany into Switzerland and unable to tell when they have crossed the border, highlights the blurriness and ultimate unimportance of the national barrier.

In contrast to the porosity of the border between nations, Renoir shows that an unbridgeable distance between the film's two principal characters—the aristocrat Boeldieu (Pierre Fresnay) and the middle-class Maréchal (Jean Gabin)—remains firmly entrenched despite many months being confined together. They are on friendly terms, but they never evince an emotional bond. At one point, Maréchal questions Boeldieu's continued use of the formal "vous" form when addressing him, and Boeldieu responds that he doesn't speak informally even with his immediate family. Though both Boeldieu and

Maréchal are French, a class antagonism divides them. But it doesn't divide Boeldieu from the aristocratic German officer von Rauffenstein (Eric von Stroheim). Von Rauffenstein holds Boeldieu prisoner, but he treats him with the utmost respect at all times and goes so far as to refuse to search his sleeping area for tools that might be used in an escape. When Boeldieu is dying, von Rauffenstein lies at his bedside and comforts as he would a close friend, even though Boeldieu is his nation's enemy. Renoir betrays some nostalgia for the dying aristocracy in his positive portraits of Boeldieu and Rauffenstein, but he sees the inevitability of their disappearance along with the appeal of the democratic Maréchal, who is finally the film's hero.[17] Simply by highlighting the intransigence of class antagonism, *La Grande Illusion* challenges the preoccupation with national identity and reveals its ideological role in obscuring class division.

Renoir makes *La Grande Illusion* not to condemn war or to highlight the stupidity of war. The antiwar film is an impossible genre, as Renoir is fully aware, and always ends up allowing spectators to find enjoyment in the war that the film criticizes. Instead, he creates a film that attempts to counter the nationalism that led to the First World War and that has the world on the brink of another war. By showing that class trumps nation, *La Grand Illusion* reveals to spectators that there is no France or Germany for which to fight. One might hazard the hypothesis that if enough members of the German working class had seen Renoir's film, they would have joined a party that eschewed nationalism rather than one that identified itself with the greatness of the nation.[18]

Like *La Grande Illusion*, *The Rules of the Game* depicts different classes in proximity with each other.[19] The film creates this proximity by focusing, after some early scenes in Paris, on a long weekend party at the country estate of Marquis Robert de La Chesnaye (Marcel Dalio) and his spouse Christine (Nora Gregor). The party at the estate La Colinière brings together various members of the Parisian upper class along with their servants. One sees, for instance, the attitudes of Christine and her maid Lisette (Paulette Dubost), as well as the interactions of the wealthy guests in juxtaposition with the interactions between their servants. During the weekend party, a variety of sexual intrigues play themselves out, and the film concludes with the death of the aviator André Jurieu, who is the key figure in the depiction of the class divide. André is neither a member of the upper class nor a servant. He displays physical heroism through his flying, but he is not a heroic figure.

The clearest contrast with *La Grande Illusion* seems to be the character of the upper class depicted in *The Rules of the Game*. In the earlier film, Boeldieu and Rauffenstein display authentic heroism despite foreseeing the disappearance of their class and thus of the ethic they uphold. Even though history definitively takes the side of Maréchal, Renoir's film remains genuinely divided in its depiction. At no point in the film do we see Boeldieu and Rauffenstein evincing corruption or decadence, but the upper-class characters in *The Rules of the Game* rarely evince anything except corruption or decadence. They never demonstrate nobility of character. Their wealth leads to the freedom to commit indiscretions without consequences rather than to a belief in their own superiority of character. Boeldieu and Rauffenstein would see in them the disappearance of the values that have defined their class.[20] Renoir's later film certainly distances itself from the upper class, but it doesn't do so in order to side with the lower class that it depicts.[21]

In the almost immediate aftermath of *La Grande Illusion*, the most striking fact of *The Rules of the Game* is how little class matters. Though there are differences in behavior among different classes—no one from the upper class shoots a gun at random within the château, for example—the differences are quantitative rather than qualitative. In general, the same motivations drive characters across class boundaries, and these motivations almost always involve the transgression of moral boundaries that exist in the society. Everyone seems committed to violating the same constraints, and this commitment provides a unity across the class divide that animates in *The Rules of the*

*Game*, which contrasts the film dramatically with *La Grande Illusion*. The sole reason for the existence of rules of the game in *The Rules of the Game* appears to be for breaking them—and in doing so, adhering to the unwritten rules of the game. And the servants find as much enjoyment in this activity as the masters.

# Rules that can never be stated

Renoir's film foregrounds the question of the title's significance since it leaves this question constantly in abeyance. It isn't clear whether the characters in the film are obeying the rules of the game or disobeying them. They largely follow social conventions, which we could construe as obedience, but they deceive, have affairs, and even acquiesce in the cover-up of a murder. These activities bespeak disobedience, which creates the uncertainty. This uncertainty is grounded in an even more important one. While characters allude at various times to the rules of the game, Renoir never makes the significance of the title directly apparent. We never know with any certainty what the rules are or even what the game is. This absence has a structuring effect in the film and orients the spectator's desire. It leads the spectator to see rules where one would not expect to see them. One watches trying to discern the elusive rules of the game, and even at the end of the film, it is not easy to formulate them.

As a result, it is very clear that the rules of the game to which the title refers are not explicit rules. One cannot find them in legal pronouncements, religious documents, or even in books about proper etiquette. Instead, these rules are necessarily implicit and unstated, though everyone in the society understands them. Adherence to the unwritten rules, much more than obedience to the written law itself, creates the social bond and enthralls subjects to the constraints inherent in this bond. The social order controls subjects through its deployment of the unwritten rules, and consequently, it does everything possible to keep these rules unarticulated and obscure.

The unwritten rules change more rapidly than written ones, and they vary within different parts of the social order. The unwritten rules might focus on sexuality among adolescents and race among adults, or language in one region of the country and dress in another. But if a social order coheres, it must have some unwritten rules that bind all members. This was clearly the case in American society during the Cold War. In order to belong to this society, one had to view the Soviet Union as an existential threat to the United States, and one had to accede to all the rituals (like bomb drills at schools) that perpetuated and exacerbated the power of the threat. Even those who disobeyed the society's written laws—that is, criminals—accepted this unwritten rule.[22] Crime leads to prison, but it doesn't lead to social exile in the way that violating the unwritten rules does. The demand for obedience to them is never articulated but is nonetheless categorical.

Most popular works of art, even when they question the formal social law, heed the unwritten rules that enable society to cohere. This is one reason why they can become popular. For instance, Kevin Costner's *Dances with Wolves* (1990) was a great popular and critical success (winning seven Academy Awards, including Best Picture). It achieved this success despite showing the genocidal actions of the American government toward the Sioux in the later part of the nineteenth century. The film remains palatable because it combines this critique with adherence to the unwritten rules of American society. The Sioux have a bond with the land that the invading whites lack, and this absence of alienation leads to the main character, Lieutenant Dunbar (Kevin Costner), becoming an adoptive member of the Sioux people. This decisive act of the film reveals how completely Costner accepts the prevailing fantasmatic image of Indians. The fantasmatic idea of their natural status as a people facilitates both their apotheosis and their annihilation. The white American who idealizes the Indians for being in touch with the natural world is the necessary supplement to the soldier who wipes them out. Both accept the fantasmatic image of Indians that affords them no place within modernity. Acceptance of this fantasy was an unwritten rule of nineteenth-century American society and remains one in the twenty-first century.

No one publicly says that one must accept this fantasy, and yet it is requisite. Accepting the fantasmatic image of Indians as unalienated and existentially linked to the natural world is an unwritten rule of contemporary American society, and *Dances with Wolves* propagates it in the guise of a critique, which enables the spectator to indulge in obedience to the unwritten rules while experiencing this obedience as transgressive. Cinematic success often correlates to an acceptable critique married with an obedience of the unwritten rules.

But *Dances with Wolves*, despite its initial popular and critical success, has not aged well. No one would now list it among the greatest films of all time, and this is not because of hidden aesthetic flaws in the film that the intervening years have brought to light. Instead, the reason lies in its utter obedience to American society's unwritten rules. The apparent radicality of the film now seems clearly a mask for an underlying adherence to the rules of the game. Popular films often transgress the written laws of a social order, but they seldom violate the unwritten rules and achieve popularity. But the trajectory of a masterpiece is often the opposite.

Great films like *The Rules of the Game*, *Citizen Kane*, and *Vertigo* (Alfred Hitchcock 1958) do not depict open acts of disobedience, like a white soldier opting to commit treason and fight against his own army on the side of the Sioux. But they receive a frosty critical and popular reception because they challenge the unwritten rules of the society rather than its written law. *Citizen Kane* not only rejects but also exposes the fundamental vacuity of capitalist accumulation, and *Vertigo* unravels the male fantasy that lies at the heart of the ideal of romance. In each case, the challenge to the unwritten rules creates a masterpiece, but at the same time, it leads to a film that contemporary audiences and critics cannot embrace.

This is also what occurs with *The Rules of the Game*, which adopts a trajectory completed opposed to that of *Dances with Wolves* or other films that depict the transgression of written laws and the acceptance of the unwritten rules. Renoir creates a film that shows both the power and the corrosiveness of the unwritten rules of the game. Though Renoir understands their social necessity, he also sees how they inhibit subjects from following their desire or from standing up against injustice. Society's unwritten rules are ultimately paralyzing politically, and exposing them is an attempt to break out of the paralysis.

Renoir leaves these rules implicit in the film in order to illustrate how their power derives from this implicitness. To state them would disguise how they function. But the film makes evident how the unwritten rules guide the characters at almost every moment. Even the apparent outsiders adhere to the rules of the game, and this is perhaps Renoir's most important insight in the film.

# The fundamental rule

Of all the unwritten rules that Renoir shows, there is one that provides the foundation for all the others: one must not allow anything to disrupt everyday life. Whereas other unwritten rules vary from society to society, this one runs across societal barriers and provides the support for all the other rules. The social order aims at reproducing itself, and it does so chiefly not through written laws or ideological demands but through the unwritten rule that ensures the dampening of any disruption. At every point in *The Rules of the Game*, characters integrate whatever disturbance that occurs into the flow of events and in this way mute any effect of the disturbance. But the formal greatness of the film lies in its ability to put the spectator in exactly the same position. As a spectator, one doesn't want the disturbance to interrupt the spectacle, and Renoir forces one to confront this desire during the film.

The demand to keep the wheels of society turning in spite of any disturbance holds even during radical shifts in governmental power. In his *Seminar VII: The Ethics of Psychoanalysis*, Lacan theorizes the role that the fundamental unwritten rule plays in terms of work. He states,

> What is Alexander's proclamation when he arrived in Persepolis or Hitler's when he arrived in Paris? The preamble isn't important: "I have come to liberate you from this or that." The essential point is "Carry on working. Work must go on." Which of course, means: "Let it be clear to everyone that this is on no account the moment to express the least surge of desire."
> The morality of power, of the service of goods, is as follows: "As far as desires are concerned, come back later. Make them wait."[23]

What Lacan refers to here as a "surge of desire" is a disruption of the everyday working of the symbolic structure. The morality that he describes here is not confined to tyrants like Alexander or Hitler but applies to every social order that privileges the promotion of the social good—that is, every social order. Keeping the social order functioning trumps any other concerns because its functioning enables subjects to believe that it provides a stable ground for their actions. As long as things appear to be running smoothly, the society takes on the guise of having a substantial existence that it doesn't really have. If society is substantial, subjects have nothing to worry about because it works regardless of their activity. This is why the image of a substantial society represents a political danger.

In order for society to appear to run on its own, subjects must turn a blind eye to what disturbs them psychically. The most stunning aspect of *The Rules of the Game* is the capacity for forgiveness that almost every character evinces. Given the ubiquity of forgiveness, it appears as if the film is an exposition of Christianity, despite the absence of any religious reference anywhere within it. But these signs of forgiveness are misleading. Characters forgive those who try to steal their spouses or try to kill them not because they are exemplars of a Christian ethic but because they heed the foundational unwritten rule of society: they want the society to run smoothly, and this is more important to them than any psychic injury that they may have received.

The key to the smooth running of the society is widespread cynicism. The cynical subject never registers any disruption of the social order's functioning. In *The Rules of the Game*, what appears as Christian charity is actually cynical distance. Cynicism renders the characters completely docile in the face of society's unwritten rules. They act as if the rules don't matter, and this distance enables them to obey without avowing that they are obeying.

The most apparently genuine characters in the film, like Christine, exhibit just as much cynicism in their actions as the most overtly cynical, like Robert. Christine sees Robert and Geneviève (Mila Parély) kissing after the hunt and comes to Geneviève's room in the château to speak with her. Rather than reprove her rival for having an affair with her husband, Christine talks with Geneviève about Robert's faults—his inability to keep a secret and his smoking in bed. When Christine sees the kiss, she initially registers its traumatic impact through her distraught look. Even though it is apparent that seeing evidence of the affair wounds Christine at the time, her quick recovery and show of friendship with her rival reveal that Robert's infidelity does not really disturb her—or she doesn't allow the disturbance to matter. She never becomes nonplused because she remains, like all the characters in the film, detached from the events that impact her directly. This cynical detachment gets the better of every dispute that the film recounts.

The most violent hostility that we see in the film occurs between the game warden Schumacher (Gaston Modot) and the poacher Marceau (Julien Carette). Marceau seduces Schumacher's wife Lisette, and in return, Schumacher chases

Marceau through the château trying to kill him. But at the end of the film after Robert has fired both of them from his staff, they forge a bond together. Renoir shows Marceau walking away from the château in a tracking shot, and Marceau stops when he spots Schumacher leaning against a tree while crying over the loss of Lisette and his job. As they talk about their respective futures, they don't dwell at all on what each has done to the other, despite the fact that each is directly responsible for the misery of the other.

Eventually, Marceau helps Schumacher spy on Christine and Octave (Jean Renoir) as they walk to the greenhouse, kiss, and plan to run away together. He facilitates the misrecognition of Christine as Lisette, and then he suggests that Schumacher shoot Octave. Marceau and Schumacher evince none of their former hostility and conspire together as what Schumacher himself calls an "équipe" (team). In order to show their newfound amity, Renoir places them together in the frame whenever they appear during this sequence. They are a team in the visual field. By doing this, Renoir involves the spectator in their bond and in the forgetting of the violence involved in their previous interaction. Marceau and Schumacher can form a team because, even as outcasts, they share an investment in keeping the social order running. But they are not exceptional: no one in the film betrays this investment.

This becomes even clearer with the death of André at the end of the film. When Schumacher shoots and kills André outside the château, no one treats this event as a crime that might require an interruption of everyday activity. Instead, the shooting has the status of an everyday event, and Robert's speech to the crowd has the effect of containing and erasing any potential disruptiveness. He announces to the crowd,

Messieurs, il s'agit d'un déplorable accident et rien de plus. Mon garde Schumacher a cru voir un braconnier et il a tiré, comme c'était son droit. La fatalité a voulu que André Jurieu soit victime de cette erreur. Messieurs, demain nous quitterons le château en pleurant cet ami exquis, ce companion de qualité qui avait su si bien nous faire oublier qu'il était un homme célèbre. Et maintenant, mes chers amis, il fait froîd. Vous risquez de prendre un mal. Je me permets de vous conseiller de rentrer. Demain nous rendrons notre devoir à notre ami Jurieu.(Sirs, it is a question of a deplorable accident and nothing more. My warden Schumacher believed that he saw a poacher and he fired, as was his right. Fate had it that André Jurieu was the victim of this error. Sirs, tomorrow we will leave the château to mourn this exquisite friend, this companion of quality who knew so well how to make us forget that he was a famous man. And now, my dear friends, it's cold. You risk catching cold. Permit me to advise you to come in. Tomorrow we will render our duty to our friend Jurieu.)[24]

Robert's statement operates on a number of levels. Most importantly, he eliminates the crime. Schumacher had an "accident" when he killed André; he did not commit murder. This distinction permits all the characters to return to their private concerns with the assurance that the social order remains intact. But he also offers a homage to André that obscures his rivalry with Robert for Christine's affection. And finally, he urges the guests to return to normal life in order to avoid the (obviously minimal) dangers of illness. This final gesture underlines the cynical function of the speech. Robert is the vehicle for the triumph of the fundamental unwritten rule of society at the end of the film.

While Robert articulates his speech about André's death, the film focuses solely on him in front of the guests with the entrance to the château behind him. It is as if Robert is speaking on stage to an audience. The audience is not only the guests assembled on the steps in front of him in the diegetic reality but also the spectator, who is implicated with the guests in the function of Robert's speech. The scene has this theatrical look in order to highlight that this is a performance, a performance designed to minimize the disruptiveness of the murder that Robert's servant has just committed.

According to Stanley Cavell's famous interpretation in the epilogue to *The World Viewed*, this scene evinces the end of Robert's game and the beginning of a different one. Cavell emphasizes the failure of Robert's speech because he doesn't look at it in terms of society's unwritten rules. Cavell writes, "In tacitly accepting the gamekeeper back into his service and thereby conspiring to cover the accident, the Marquis places himself at the mercy of the gamekeeper. In explicitly accepting the gun as the lawful defense of his domain (i.e., his domain inside the house, his private life), he has submitted himself to the gun's dominion."[25] Cavell sees a loss of Robert's authority occurring in the final scene at the exact moment when Robert asserts his authority. This interpretation isolates Robert's actions at the end from his actions throughout the film, and it gives Schumacher way too much credit. Robert displays this loss of authority throughout the film, and he loses authority not to a specific figure like Schumacher or the gun but to the unwritten rule that he obeys when minimizing the effect of André's murder.

The film doesn't depict a technological or class revolution that deprives a former authority of his authority.[26] Instead, it lays bare the absence of revolution. What stands out about this absence is the belief that the characters in this world have in their own ability to revolt and succeed in revolting. They see themselves as free to transgress whatever societal restriction they come up against. But the image of revolutionary action substitutes for revolutionary action. Schumacher cannot displace Robert because Robert has already displaced himself through his obedience of the fundamental unwritten rule, an obedience that his final speech merely confirms.

In the face of the fundamental unwritten rule, neither the representative of the past (Robert) nor the representative of the future (André) stands a chance. At the moment they try to assert their authority, they end up indicating their capitulation to the dominance of this rule. At no point in *The Rules of the Game* does anyone effectuate a sustained escape from its dominance. But by drawing the spectator's attention to it, Renoir gives the spectator some purchase on the power that it has.

# A world of accidents

When Robert provides the justification for Schumacher's shooting of André, he characterizes it as an "accident" rather than a murder. In addition to mitigating the disruptiveness of the event, his choice of words has a larger significance for the film as a whole. The accident plays a central role in the film: every major event has an accidental status: Schumacher shooting André, Christine seeing Robert and Genvière kissing, André crashing his car, Octave ending up in the greenhouse with Christine, and so on. In *The Rules of the Game*, the accident wholly replaces the act.

There are only accidents in *The Rules of the Game* because characters wholly enthralled to the unwritten rules of the society are unable to act. The unwritten rules act through subjects, and thus their acts appear as accidents. And yet, Renoir suggests that this doesn't absolve the subject of responsibility. When one watches the film, one watches a series of accidents, but they have subjects who perpetuate them. In this way, the film confronts a modern world where accidents have replaced acts and reinterprets the accident as a new version of the act.

This insight of *The Rules of the Game* into the prevalence of the accident mirrors one of the important insights of psychoanalysis. In his second major work published just after *The Interpretation of Dreams*, Freud takes up the role that the accident has for the psyche. *The Psychopathology of Everyday Life* discusses acts of forgetting, errors in reading, slips of the tongue—all forms of accident that befall subjects—in order to show that the accident is usually not just an accident.[27] It also provides an opportunity for the unconscious to express itself. In fact, Freud argues that the unconscious expresses itself primarily through accidents. This demands not only that we pay more attention to accidents but that we grasp our unconscious responsibility for them.

The task of psychoanalysis is that of enabling the subject to assume responsibility for the accidents that befall it. This is what separates psychoanalysis from other forms of therapy that attempt to offer solace or to relieve the subject of experiencing too much responsibility. Even though the very idea of an accident suggests that no one is responsible, sustaining freedom in the modern world requires a connection between the accident and the subject's desire. In a world where accidents replace acts, we must locate the subject's freedom in the accident. Otherwise, the subject is just a victim of what happens to it. *The Rules of the Game* exhibits characters who believe they are the victims of accidents, but the film shows the spectator the responsibility that the characters bear for these accidents. In the diegetic reality, accidents proliferate, but an accident is never just an accident.

It is significant that the last lines of dialogue in the film involve the word "accident." After Robert justifies the death of André as an accident, Saint-Aubin (Pierre Nay) and the Général (Pierre Magnier) have a brief discussion of this interpretation of the event. In one sense, it is just untrue to say that André's death was an accident. Robert lies to cover up a crime. Schumacher was trying to kill someone, and he succeeded in doing so. But the fact that André died rather than Octave was accidental, and the fact that Schumacher imagined that he saw Octave kissing Lisette rather than Christine in the greenhouses was an accidental misrecognition.

Not persuaded by Robert's slanted version of the events, Saint-Aubin says to the Général, "Une nouvelle définition du mot 'accident'" (A new definition of the word "accident"). But the Général reproves him and expresses admiration for Robert's adherence to the fundamental rule. He says, "Non, non, non, non, non. Ce La Chesnaye ne manque pas de classe, et ça devient rare, mon cher Saint-Aubin, croyez-moi, ça devient rare" (No, no, no, no, no. This La Chesnaye has class, and that's becoming rare, my dear Saint-Aubin, believe me, that's becoming rare). The Général interprets Robert's employment of the term "accident" as a sign of connection with an aristocratic tradition and that tradition's ability to preserve appearances. But what his conclusion fails to see—and what the film emphasizes—is that the rise of the accident testifies to the emergence of a modern world in which traditional agency has disappeared.

The use of the term "accident" has the effect of lifting the blame for the event from the perpetuator. If Schumacher's murder of André is an accident, he is not a murderer. The film does show that André's death was indeed an accident because Schumacher means to kill Octave rather than André, but it also indicates that in the act of killing André, Schumacher realizes the desire that animates him throughout the film. He wants to preserve the rules of the game, and his final act does so through the elimination of André and his potential disruption of these rules. The accident is thus not wholly a chance occurrence, even though it escapes Schumacher's conscious intention.

The question of the accident is the fundamental question that the film poses. The film concludes with this discussion of the accident in order to highlight its ontological importance in the modern world. When the unwritten rules have the power that they do, agency disappears into accidents. There is no possible escape from the world of the accident, but Renoir compels the spectator to interpret the accident as a manifestation of the unconscious. In this sense, the justification of a killing as an accident in no way relieves the perpetuator of responsibility. The subject is responsible for its unconscious and the accidents it produces. The ethical challenge of modernity lies in confronting subjects with this responsibility, and *The Rules of the Game* plays a part in this same struggle.

## Everyone on board

When viewing *The Rules of the Game*, one of the central questions concerns who doesn't understand or follow the unwritten rules. Who is the exception? The structure of the film leads us to believe in various exceptions, but it subsequently reveals their lack of exceptionality. Renoir does this in order to demonstrate just how far the power of the society's unwritten rules extends. The first apparent exception is André, and his exceptionality manifests itself through the form of the film.

The film begins with André landing in Paris after a successful transatlantic flight and publicly proclaiming to a radio interviewer his disappointment that Christine is not present to greet him. The problem with this proclamation on the radio is that it brings André's private love affair with the married Christine into the public. The upper class permits and even encourages such indiscretions as long as they remain private, but André's public voicing of his affection for Christine violates this unstated prohibition and attests to his displacement among the French upper class. It seems as if André's misstep in the film's first minutes indicates the direction that *The Rules of the Game* will go—toward the emphasis on class antagonism articulated in *La Grande Illusion*. André's failure to distinguish between what one can discuss privately and what one can say publicly separates him as a figure who has just entered the upper class from the other characters in the film firmly entrenched in the upper class. Renoir emphasizes his disruptive force formally when André first appears on screen.

The opening shot of the film is a tracking shot that begins by following a microphone wire and then continues following the radio reporter (Lise Elina) as she reports on André's flight and walks toward his plane as it lands. Renoir cuts from the tracking shot to the image of the plane landing, which indicates André's disruption of the aesthetic continuity of the film and, metaphorically, the disruption that he occasions relative to the other characters in the film. André's transatlantic flight intrudes in the visual field just as he intrudes later at the weekend party. Immediately afterward, this disruptiveness manifests itself in the film's content as André's friend Octave greets him with the news that Christine is not there. As André articulates his disappointment to Octave, the radio reporter emerges between them in the shot and begins to interview André about his achievement. The private conversation between André and Octave bleeds into the public interview, and André states his disappointment with Christine for the entire nation to hear. He doesn't understand the rule of the game: one can love a married woman, but one must keep quiet publicly about the liaison. André's misstep that opens the film leads most commentators to believe that he is the titular character, the one who violates the rules of the game. But this is to proceed much too quickly and to accept the beginning of the film as the final word.

Renoir places André in this position to emphasize his difference from the other characters in the film, but this difference subsequently evaporates when André joins the party at the country estate of Robert and Christine, La Colinière. Octave makes a special plea to Robert for André's inclusion, and Robert's agreement offers the first indication that André is not the exception that he appears to be. André comes to the party determined to proclaim his love for Christine to Robert and to take Christine away from him. But when the opportunity arises for André to leave with Christine, he ruins his chances because he believes that he must act according to a code of honor and confront Robert prior to leaving. When he informs Christine that they cannot sneak away without telling Robert, he says to her, "Ça se fait" (That's how it's done). More than anything else André says or does, this statement reveals his obedience to society's unwritten rules that he seems to violate in the film's opening scene.

Through his code of heroism, Renoir links André's initial disruptiveness to obedience. Heroism functions as a rule of the game for him. As Octave tells Christine, André believes himself to be a hero and must always act the part. In this way, the film reveals that André, despite his violations of certain unspoken rules of the game, remains enthralled to other rules of the game. André is not the disruptive force that he appears to be, and his actions confirm the stranglehold that the unwritten rules of the game have even on outsiders.

After the initial suggestion that André is the character out of touch with the rules of the game, Renoir shows that no one in the film is immune to these rules.[28] This conformity isn't the result of a series of conscious decisions but unconscious investments in social authority. Everyone desires to be an insider because that is where enjoyment appears to lie. Even the outsider André soon shows himself to be an insider of a different type. André doesn't belong to the society of La Colinière, but he does belong to one that demands that heroes act according to a strict code of honor. His initial act of disobedience turns out to be a disguised obedience to another set of rules that Renoir only makes apparent after the fact. The spectator sees an initial act of transgression, but subsequently this act loses its transgressive quality and becomes instead a mark of an investment in the symbolic law rather than a disregard for it. Renoir withholds information from the spectator concerning André's obedience in order for the spectator to succumb to the initial illusion of transgression. By beginning with this illusion and then exposing it as such, the film indicates the broad reach of the rules of the game into the very terrain that appears to mark their rejection.

Other characters follow this same trajectory in the film. As much as André, the game warden Schumacher seems to flaunt the rules of the game. When he sees Marceau sneaking around with his wife Lisette, Schumacher begins to pursue him through the estate. He even fires on him repeatedly with his gun inside the château, despite the presence of many guests. Though no stray bullet hits an unlucky bystander, Schumacher's actions lead the Marquis to dismiss him from his employment toward the end of the film.

On the one hand, the events with Schumacher suggest that the servants act just like the masters. Lisette has a lover who parallels Christine's, and Schumacher is jealous and wants to keep his wife just like Robert. On the other hand, Schumacher's reaction is much more extreme than that of Robert. The Marquis acquiesces to his wife's departure even though it dismays him, and he certainly doesn't take up arms against André as Schumacher does against Marceau. It appears that Schumacher doesn't understand the unwritten rules of the game—that one commits and tolerates infidelity as long as it remains hidden from public view.

When Robert fires Schumacher for his antics during the party, his exclusion seems definitive. But after Schumacher actually kills someone rather than just shooting at him, Robert welcomes him back into the fold and explains away his crime as a mere accident. This final inclusion of Schumacher suggests that, as is the case with André, his violation of the rules of the game was only apparent. As psychoanalysis shows, explicit disobedience often masks unconscious obedience. Despite shooting and killing a guest on his master's estate, Schumacher still belongs to the community. His seeming disobedience turns out to be a disguised form of obedience because it assists the Marquis in keeping up appearances.

Just as Schumacher belongs, so do all the servants. The link between the servant class and the rules of the game becomes most pronounced in the case of Lisette. Like Christine, Lisette has lovers to whom she turns when she is away from her husband. In their first scene together in the film, Christine questions Lisette about her lovers, and Lisette reveals that her morality is no different from that of the upper class. But more importantly, Lisette is the force that upholds the existing social relations at the end of the film when Octave prepares to flee together with Christine. Lisette is the character who tells Octave that a relationship with Christine would be doomed to failure, and her intervention leads him to change his mind and send André to Christine rather than returning to her himself.

Renoir depicts the investment of the servants in the social game not to mute the class critique of the film but to show how extensively ideology reaches. As the film makes clear, the role of the servant is not ensuring the mastery of the master but confirming the master's position within the ideological system of the social order. At the moment when someone would violate the operative ideological imperative or depart from the rules of the game, a servant intervenes in order to bring this would-be dissident back into line. Renoir scathingly depicts the capitulation of the wealthy to the ideological demands of their society, but he refuses to romanticize the servants as immune to these same demands. Ideology continues to function through those whom it deprives of status.

The role that the servants play in *The Rules of the Game* is crucial to the film's achievement. This depiction reveals that even those denigrated by the rules of the game invest themselves in these rules and find enjoyment through them. The servants aren't on the verge of rebellion because servitude offers them a sense of belonging, and the vehicle for this belonging is the society's unwritten rules. The investment in these rules prevents the servants from being exceptional.

The lower class in *The Rules of the Game* contrasts clearly with the lower class in Renoir's other French films of the mid- and late 1930s, the so-called Popular Front films. For example, *The Lower Depths* associates the lower class with freedom in the case of the Baron (Louis Jouvet), who finds emancipation when he abandons his aristocratic life for a flophouse, and in *A Day in the Country*, Henriette (Sylvia Bataille) escapes from the banality of her middle-class life through an encounter with a working-class man. The lower class no longer provides a site for freedom in *The Rules of the Game*. One might hypothesize that Renoir abandons his earlier devotion to the class struggle. But this conclusion would miss how the film extends the critique of the earlier films. In this later film, Renoir takes stock of how the social order produces a psychic investment even among those it oppresses and thus struggles against the barrier that this investment poses.

# Parallel exclusions

The social order offers enjoyment to subjects through a sense of belonging, but one can only belong if others don't. Even though there are no exceptions in *The Rules of the Game*, there are exclusions. Exclusion is the condition of possibility for enjoying one's obedience to the society's unwritten rules. The exclusion of those who don't belong gives this obedience a significance. One never feels like one belongs as much as at the moment when another is excluded.

Symbolic identity has no substantial status, and it exists only through the action that distinguishes it. This is why symbolic identity depends on exclusion. No one can belong unless there is a distinct group that one joins, and if the distinction lies just in a positive characteristic that anyone can have, then the group is not really distinct. Exclusion creates the distinctiveness of the group that allows it to confer symbolic identity on its members. One invests through a commitment to the exclusions that those in the group share.

The parallel between the masters and the servants stems from their joint investment in the rules of the game, and this includes an investment in the exclusions that separate those who can play the game from those who can't. The rules of the game offer enjoyment for those who obey them but only insofar as there are those who aren't permitted to play. Renoir depicts this aspect of the parallel midway through the film by juxtaposing a discussion among the servants eating dinner with a conversation that occurs in the hallway among the guests at La Colinière. The servants impugn Robert for his Jewish heritage, and even the chef (Léon Larive) who defends him comments solely on Robert's good taste rather than condemning anti-Semitism. No one among the servants calls into question the basic assumptions underlying the initial anti-Semitic remark.

Renoir cuts from this dinner scene to a scene upstairs where the masters are preparing to go to their rooms for the night. The way that he transitions from one scene to the next leaves no doubt about their connection. As the servants continue talking, he cuts to a close-up of the radio that plays background music, but this shot of the radio quickly dissolves into a shot of the clock upstairs that chimes in the background of the conversation among the masters. The graphic match of the radio and the clock indicates that a parallel background exists for both groups, and the conversation that ensues among the masters reveals that they share similar assumptions about who belongs and who doesn't.

While no character simply repeats the anti-Semitism displayed among the servants, we do see a bald expression of racism. Madame de la Bruyère (Claire Gérard) questions Jackie (Anne Mayen) about the nature of pre-Columbian civilization that she knows Jackie is studying. When Jackie explains that it is American civilization prior to the arrival of Columbus, Madame de la Bruyère responds, "O, c'est l'histoire des nègres" (Oh, the history of Negroes). Jackie corrects her by noting that this history concerns Indians rather than "Negroes," and Madame de la Bruyère concludes the conversation by grouping the Indians under the category of "Buffalo Bill." Madame de la Bruyère's racist conflation of black and Indian, followed by her equation of Indians with Buffalo Bill, is not identical to the anti-Semitism on display during the servants' dinner. Renoir does show a difference between the servants and the masters concerning whom they exclude. But he juxtaposes these two scenes to illustrate how little this difference matters: only a different focus, not a fundamentally different attitude, separates the two groups when it is a question of their joint commitment to important social exclusions.

More than any other sequence in the film, the juxtaposition of the exchange between the servants and the related exchange between the masters indicates the similarity that resides within their difference. Even though they have contrasting codes that govern how they speak to each other and how they conduct their lives, they share an investment in certain unwritten rules that demand the exclusion that enable their society to achieve an imaginary coherence. As much as a democratic spectator might like to believe it, the servants are not less invested in these rules than the masters.[29] In *The Rules of the Game*, there are no outsiders, and Renoir specifically produces this absence as an indictment of the spectator's capitulation to rules that govern with silent impunity and silent destructiveness.[30]

# Democracy and depth of field

The great formal gesture of *The Rules of the Game*—Renoir's use of depth of field for both interior and exterior shots—seems to have nothing to do with society's unwritten rules.[31] But, in fact, Renoir manages to transform even this technique into a tool for displaying the dominance of the unwritten rules. In his hands, deep focus becomes not just a way of expanding the visual field but also a way of exposing how the psychic investment in the unwritten rules extends across all social barriers.

Filmmakers use deep focus in order to extend the range of visibility and give the spectator more to see. When a filmmaker does not use depth of field for a shot, certain elements in the shot form an undistinguished background for other elements that become prominent. This disjunction between foreground and background doesn't disappear with depth of field, but depth gives the background more importance relative to the foreground than it has when the focus is only on the foreground. In this sense, depth of field represents a democratic approach to the material within the shot. The characters and objects in the background count in the visual field rather than just being incidental to the characters and objects in the foreground. It equalizes everything that we see.

According to André Bazin, the great champion of depth of field in the cinema, deep focus doesn't only provide a more democratic visual field for the characters within it but also creates a more democratic cinema for the spectator. For Bazin, deep focus represents a political choice by the filmmaker.[32] Whereas montage directs the spectator's look and thus produces passive spectatorship, depth of field demands an active spectator who can look where she or he wants to look within the image. Bazin contends that depth of field produces

> both a more active mental attitude on the part of the spectator and a more positive contribution on his part to the action in progress. While analytical montage only calls

for him to follow his guide, to let his attention follow along smoothly with that of the director who will choose what he should see, here he is called upon to exercise at least a minimum of personal choice.[33]

Even if one doesn't accept Bazin's apotheosis of depth entirely, his basic point that its use places more agency in the hands of the spectator seems indisputable.

The democratic equalizing of the field of vision that occurs through the use of depth of field manifests itself throughout *The Rules of the Game*. Renoir employs deep focus to give equal space to the servants, to allow the spectator to see what the servants are doing while the masters are doing something else. The most common deep focus shot in the film occurs in the long hallway of the château. In this hallway, we see characters interact at various levels in the shot. Just before the guests go to their rooms for the night, shots of the hallway in deep focus depict masters and servants equally visible though separated spatially.

In one such shot, Octave and Christine occupy the foreground on the left side of the image, while Robert is talking with a guest in the middle of the background. Both couples are in focus. In the space between them on the right side of the image, a servant is walking down the hallway. As the servant walks, he passes by without paying attention to either of the couples. Though the servant doesn't speak or play a central role in the action of the shot, the spectator sees him clearly, and he remains in focus until he walks out of the scene. Renoir gives the servant a visual significance that he otherwise wouldn't have through the use of deep focus in this shot. But at the same time that the servant's visual inclusion reveals his equality with the masters, it also reveals that he shares their investment in the society's unwritten rules. The fact that we can see both masters and servants in focus in all the shots reveals that the servants are not just the background against which the masters act. They are fully part of the social order depicted, just as they are fully in focus in the shots.

The visual belonging of the servants becomes even more pronounced in other deep focus shots in the film, when we see masters and servants acting precisely the same in the foreground and in the background. In a later scene, we see André and Schumacher in focus at different levels of the shot while behaving in exactly the same way—engaging in an outburst of jealousy because of a woman's suspicious activity. Schumacher is no different than André, and Lisette sneaking away from her husband earlier in the background of the scene is no different than Christine having an intimate interaction with Saint-Aubin later in the background of the same scene. Depth reveals an absence of difference.

Depth of field in *The Rules of the Game* functions democratically, but in doing so, it exhibits the underside of democracy—a society in which no one doesn't fit. By making clear visually that everyone has an equal place in the filmic world, Renoir depicts the extent of everyone's investment in the unwritten rules of the social order. He uses depth of field to convey sameness rather than difference. The various levels of the shot tend to reproduce each other, not highlight differences. In this way, Renoir's employment of deep focus runs in the opposite direction from its more famous use in *Citizen Kane*, which asks the spectator to contrast the foreground and the background of the shot in order to understand relationships and differences. The activity that Renoir uses deep focus to show is a multilayered obedience from which no one escapes.

## Hunting for obedience

Deep focus plays a key role in the most famous scene in *The Rules of the Game*—the hunting scene. In these stunning few minutes, we see the servants, led by the gamekeeper Schumacher, rouse the animals that their masters subsequently shoot. The deep focus shots of the servants walking in a line through the woods and banging sticks on trees are interlaced with complementary deep focus shots of the masters taking their places and preparing to shoot. Renoir also includes shots of the different rabbits and pheasants that will become the prey of the hunters.

The scene then turns to a montage of the wealthy shooting and the animals dying. The most rapid editing during the film occurs during this shot sequence. As Alexander Sesonske points out,

> The central, shooting segment of the hunt remains, with the opening sequence of *La Bête humaine*, Renoir's primary exploitation of the power of editing. In a film whose shots often run for a minute or more, here fifty-one shots take just three minutes, forty seconds, in a mounting rhythm of cutting and movement which culminates in that awesome barrage of gunfire as, in twenty-two shots—fifty-three seconds—twelve animals die.[34]

Critics tend to see the scene as a critique of the thoughtless cruelty of the upper class, and it does show this. But it creates an investment in this cruelty. Renoir simultaneously creates sympathy for the slaughtered animals and uses the structure of the film to make the slaughter enjoyable. Even those opposed to hunting, like Renoir himself, have a psychic investment in the hunt that this scene brings to the fore.[35]

Renoir's antihunting hunting scene is impossible to imagine today. It relies for its effectiveness on the actual deaths of actual animals in order to expose the barbarism of hunting. If it were made today, the People for the Ethical Treatment of Animals (PETA) would not certify that no animals were injured in the making of this film, but the violent deaths of the animals are integral to the film's effect. The suffering of the animals exposes the cruelty not only of the upper class that Renoir depicts but also of Renoir himself as a filmmaker. In other words, Renoir has to replicate the very cruelty that he condemns in order to condemn it. This contradiction would, for a contemporary filmmaker, obviate the critique. But for Renoir, his own complicity, as well as that of the spectator, is inextricable from the critique that he authors.

By implicating Renoir himself in the critique that he authors, this scene heeds one of the most significant insights of psychoanalysis: the subject cannot exempt itself from its act of enunciation. Every statement that we make involves us in what we're talking about. We can never speak (or make a film) from a distance, which means that we cannot but contribute to the object of our critique in the very act of critiquing it. This hidden complicity doesn't destroy the possibility of critique but does complicate it and forces us to consider our own investment in what repulses us. Every critique must be a critique of the critic at the same time as the object of the critique. Our hidden complicity is the manifestation of the unconscious, and the chief virtue of the hunting scene lies in its effort to expose the unconscious within its critique.[36]

Some critics have noted that the fact that the character that Renoir plays in the film, Octave, does not carry a gun or shoot in the hunt reveals Renoir's personal objection to hunting. While this may be the case, it is also the case that Octave isn't absent from the hunting scene. Octave accompanies André throughout the scene and remains by his side as he participates in the hunt. He is not a heroic resistance fighter against the cruelty that he witnesses but rather its silent partner, as Renoir the director is as well. In effect, one should see Octave as the real target of the critique in this scene. By going along without participating, he provides a tacit justification that sustains the existence of the hunt in the same way that the spectator's enjoyment does.

The structure of the hunting scene builds suspense around the killing of the animals. Even though the spectator knows that the killing will take place, Renoir extends the time prior to it and provides multiple shots of the animals before we see any of them being shot. This delay creates anticipation in the spectator for what is to come and invests even the unwilling spectator in the killing. The delay that precedes the killing has the effect of arousing desire, and this desire is how the spectator is involved in the slaughter.

Renoir's depiction of the hunt creates suspense but completely eliminates surprise. Here, one should rely on Alfred Hitchcock's famous explanation of the distinction between suspense and surprise in order to understand how the scene functions in relation to the spectator. Suspense, according to Hitchcock, involves the filmmaker giving the spectator knowledge about what will happen and then forcing the spectator to wait for the event that she or he knows will come. Surprise, in contrast, demands that the filmmaker withhold knowledge in order to produce the effect.[37] Too much knowledge would, obviously, spoil the surprise. Hitchcock privileges suspense over surprise because it holds the spectator for a longer time, but it also involves the spectator in the events on the screen more than surprise does. But the fact that Renoir uses suspense rather than surprise to depict a hunt is itself surprising. During most actual hunts, both the hunter and the prey experience surprise—the hunter when she or he spots the target, and the prey when it finds itself struck by a bullet.

By transforming the surprise that takes place in an actual hunt into a scene stripped of any surprise, Renoir emphasizes the absence of any sport in the hunt. Hunting in the film is purely a massacre because there is no surprise, and surprise is essential to sport. We participate in and watch sports because the outcome might surprise us. Jean-Pierre Boon points out this aspect of Renoir's depiction of the hunt. He writes, "The hunt is presented not as the sport that one might expect, not as a challenge to the force, endurance, intelligence or skill of the participants, but rather as a slaughter (a beat), a massacre organized by the game warden Schumacher (Gaston Modot) for the benefit of the guests and masters of the château La Colinière."[38] The absence of any challenge in the hunt eliminates surprise and furthers the spectator's complicity in what happens. When we are surprised, we are not involved in what surprises us (which is why we can be surprised), but when we experience suspense we anticipate and expect what is to come. In a suspenseful situation, we invest ourselves in the suspense coming to fruition.

The scene begins with a shot of Saint-Aubin and La Bruyère (Richard Francoeur) walking down a path toward the camera while the latter excuses himself for shooting a pheasant that was in the range of the former. As he does often, in this scene, Renoir shoots their conversation in deep focus, so that we see clearly the group walking behind them as well. As they arrive at Robert and a group already awaiting them, the camera pans to follow them and continues to highlight the connection between all the characters in the scene through depth of field. No one is excluded from the hunt. Even those who don't take part in shooting assist in some aspect of it or simply go along with what's happening. The depth of field provides the spectator with an index of everyone's involvement.

The hunt commences in earnest when Schumacher lines up the servants to walk through the woods and beat sticks against the trees in order to direct the animals to the hunters. Renoir shoots this in a deep focus shot that includes several visual levels of servants working under Schumacher. He cuts from this shot of the servants to a parallel deep focus shot of the masters in a similar line preparing to shoot. The involvement of everyone is visually affirmed.

After depicting the beaters working through the woods, Renoir cuts to a montage of rabbits and pheasants. This montage sequence at once creates sympathy for the victims by identifying them but also points out potential targets. After cutting back to the beaters, Renoir includes a montage of the hunters that parallels that of the animals, as the hunters silently prepare to fire. Christine speaks the first dialogue that interrupts the montage, as she asks her cousin, "Jackie, tu aimes la chasse?" (Jackie, do you like hunting?). When Jackie expresses her enthusiasm for hunting and returns the question to Christine, the latter just shrugs. This anticipates her later statement to Robert that she doesn't like hunting at all. But this absence of affection doesn't prevent Christine from joining in the shooting. She follows along because she enjoys following along, not because she enjoys hunting. But this is the case even for the spectator.

After Christine's demonstration of ambivalence toward the hunt, the film returns to another lengthy shot of the beaters driving the animals out of the woods and then another montage of the animals running and flying. After several shots in the montage, a gunshot rings out, and a rabbit falls to the ground. This first gunshot by Robert unleashes a flurry of gunshots from the rest of the hunting party. The film divides its emphasis between the enjoyment of the shooters and the suffering of the victims. Some shots include both figures, while others isolate one or the other. The final death stresses the agony of a rabbit as it stretches out its paws just before dying, so that we see the price that follows from the hunters obeying the rules of the game.

The waiting period before the shooting invests the spectator in the success of the hunt. The wait aims at focusing the spectator's desire on the first shot. This gunshot becomes the object of desire in the scene. Renoir structures the film so that the spectator will both enjoy the killing of the animals and be repulsed by this slaughter at the same time. The killing is suspenseful and horrific. This contradictory formal demand is crucial to the film's effect. If the spectator could remain distanced from the hunt and simply be appalled by the hunters, the scene would become a facile moral (and ineffectual) condemnation. Moral condemnation doesn't lead to changes in behavior. In order for the film to disturb the spectator and thus have an effect, it must combine enjoyment and repulsion. This is the only way that the film can critique not just hunting but the unconscious motivation that drives us to hunt. The critique continues in the aftermath of the hunt, which is in some sense more unrelenting than the hunt itself.

When the hunt concludes, no one evinces any pleasure in what they have done. In fact, Robert has so little interest that he postpones the display of the trophies until later. As the servants and the dogs round up the dead animals, it becomes clear how little the hunt meant to its participants. Everyone participates for the sake of participating, and their enjoyment is located in the participation rather than in the event itself. By showing this to the spectator and also involving the spectator in this participation, Renoir highlights the subject's proclivity for capitulation to the unwritten rules of the game. This scene stands out in the history of cinema as perhaps the greatest enactment of the proclivity to capitulate alongside the horror that it unleashes.

# The indifference of identity

The proclivity to capitulate begins with adopting a symbolic identity. This is what Lacan calls the forced choice that inaugurates desiring subjectivity.[39] Subjects take up a symbolic identity within their social order. Their names are the most obvious manifestation of this symbolic identity, though it extends to all aspects of their social position—their gender, ethnicity, region of origin, profession, religion, class status, and so on. Symbolic identity gives a subject particular qualities through which it aligns itself and differentiates itself from other subjects. It is where we locate our singularity. But as psychoanalysis shows, this is a fundamental error. Though symbolic identity involves differences, it obscures the singularity of the subject by placing it in a framework that measures the subject through the Other or anonymous social authority. Symbolic identity gives us authorized differences that don't ultimately matter.

When we stake our singularity on symbolic identity, we define ourselves through the Other and tacitly accept the given rules of the game. But it is difficult to gain awareness of this sacrifice of one's singularity to the Other. Symbolic identity assures us that this identity is our own, even though it exists prior to our act of adopting it. Adopting a symbolic identity is the primordial form of obedience, the initial acceptance of the rules of the game, and Renoir aims at exposing this obedience in order to break its spell over us. He does this by emphasizing the interchangeability of different symbolic identities in *The Rules of the Game*.

Disguises and cases of mistaken identity appear throughout the film. But Renoir doesn't use the disguise or the case of mistaken identity to highlight an epistemological problem. Characters misidentify each other not because they lack knowledge but because the characters in the film, even those that seem the most distinct like André and Octave, are interchangeable. Anyone can become an avatar for anyone else. No one's identity is securely her or his own. This interchangeability bespeaks the unimportance of precisely the kind of differences that we prize as significant.

The killing of André at the end of the film involves a double misrecognition. As they leave the estate, Schumacher and Marceau see a couple outside, and they misidentify one of the two. Schumacher sees Christine wearing Lisette's cape while walking with Octave and assumes that she is Lisette. They initially identify Octave correctly, though another misrecognition follows after he leaves and goes into the château. He promises Christine that he will return quickly, but after a conversation with Lisette inside, he undergoes a change of heart and authorizes André to return in his place. When Schumacher shoots at the man he sees coming back to meet Christine, he believes that he is shooting Octave, but he kills André. André dies for pursuing Lisette even though he had no relationship with her at all, and he is actually pursuing Christine rather than Lisette. The double misrecognition that ends in his death reveals the interchangeability of all identities in the film. Renoir concludes with the death by mistaken identity in order to underline this absence of distinctiveness.

Renoir submits the spectator to even more confusion than exists among the characters in the filmic reality. He uses a large cast and does little to differentiate the characters from each other. The spectator's confusion about character identity is not a failure on the part of the spectator but a formal feature of the film itself. One is not supposed to be able to differentiate among the many anonymous guests or even between important characters. Renoir chooses actors that resemble each other to play some of the main roles in the film in order to foster this confusion on the part of the spectator. Differences between characters are less important than what they hold in common— their commitment to the social bond.

The indifference of symbolic difference manifests itself in the ease with which characters can move from one lover to another. Even though the film portrays Christine sympathetically, she expresses her love for three different characters and shows affection for another during the few days that the film depicts. Christine can move from Robert to André to Saint-Aubin to Octave and back to Robert because each of these characters is interchangeable for her and interchangeable in the filmic universe. Christine's capriciousness in love is not evidence of her particular failing but of the inability of any character to stand out.

Even the act of murder doesn't permit a character to stand out. Typically, murder is a way of asserting one's singularity and revolting against social constraints, but this is not the case in *The Rules of the Game*. As Christopher Faulkner contends, this distinguishes *The Rules of the Game* from Renoir's earlier films in the 1930s like *Le Crime de Monsieur Lange*. He writes,

> In the earlier films murder is an act of rebellion—the most serious social crime next to revolution—committed by a solitary protagonist, and frequently committed on behalf of some alternative social interests as well as his own. *La Règle du jeu*, on the other hand, has no individual protagonist— certainly not Schumacher—so in a very real sense its murder is committed by the prevailing social formation, although it is not the less a political murder for that.[40]

Faulkner's point that the social order itself commits the murder reflects the power that the social order has in the filmic world. There is no individuality that escapes its gravitational force.

The film exposes the absence of individuality by avoiding the imaginary lure of depth that most films succumb to. Most filmmakers aspire to the creation of complex characters that have conflicting motivations, but this is precisely what Renoir eschews in *The Rules of the Game*. Everyone acts according to the prescriptions of her or his symbolic position and heeds the unwritten rules of the social order. No one is able to deviate from the rules of the game and carve out a distinct identity.

That is to say, Renoir succeeds in creating characters without any psychology. As Pierre Guislain notes,

> With these characters, each as improbable as the other, Renoir doesn't seek to render them more credible by giving them what we call psychological thickness. Christine, Jurieu, Octave and Robert are (apparently at least) totally transparent beings. They have no secret garden, no hidden vices or qualities. Acting without any ulterior motives, always in the first degree, they say only what they think and do only what they say.[41]

The characters are nothing more than their symbolic identities. Guislain goes on to point out that this absence of depth drives the initial hostility to the film, and yet, it is precisely what Renoir is trying to accomplish. Only characters without any psychology reveal the power of the rules of the game.

# The play's the thing

When the guests first arrive at La Colinière, Robert proposes a masquerade for their amusement. The masquerade occurs after the hunt and repeats the dynamic operative in this earlier activity. Even though the hunt involves rampant killing and the masquerade concerns farcical entertainment, the tone of each scene is the same. Both activities reveal the enjoyment of Robert, Christine, and the guests. In each case, they enjoy through the symbolic role that they take up, though the masquerade makes this more evident and thus reveals the truth at work during the hunt. The characters in the film are nothing but the masks that they put on, which is why Renoir highlights the centrality of the masquerade.

But Renoir films the masquerade scene unexpectedly. He begins with a shot of the sheet music that the pianist is using to accompany the performance, pans down to the hands of the musician playing, and then pulls back to show her at the piano. The first cut in the scene turns to the action on the stage at the moment it concludes. At the beginning of the weekend, Robert proposed the masquerade as the climactic event, but Renoir deprives the spectator of this main event in which the central characters in the film—Robert, Christine, André, Octave, Saint-Aubin, Genviève, and others—all perform on stage together. After the curtain ends the performance, a long pan across the applauding and laughing crowd suggests the amount of amusement that the masquerade produced. Renoir leaves the spectator out of this amusement. Though we see subsequent acts, we don't see the main event, despite its apparent great success.

Because the audience appreciates the performance to such an extent, they call for an encore, and the performers, with the exception of Christine and Saint-Aubin, oblige. In direct contrast to the original performance, we see the encore directly, which draws attention to the absence of the original. Renoir provides us with the sequel rather than the original in order to underline the film's emphasis on theatricality and performance. It is the copy that retroactively constitutes the original, and there is no original prior to its theatrical duplication. Even the performance is a copy of a performance.

Just before the encore begins, Christine and Saint-Aubin sneak away, presumably to have a sexual liaison. The cover of the performance facilitates their escape and paralyzes André from preventing it. Even though André seems uncomfortable on the stage, unlike the other characters, he nonetheless has an investment in the performance and cannot just abandon it to keep an eye on Christine. And it is his commitment to the performance that paves the way for Christine's infidelity. As the performance continues, it also distracts Schumacher from Lisette and Marceau, allowing them to try to escape from his surveillance. But in the end, there is no escaping, because performance is ubiquitous in the filmic world. Even lovers don't escape the fact of performance when they retreat from the actual performances.

The film insists that there is no space outside the stage, that performance has a constitutive role in relation to identity. As Karla Oeler points out, the whole diegetic world of *The Rules of the Game* is theatrical. It is a world in which there is only a stage. Oeler writes, "With *The Rules of the Game*, the division between onstage and off, inclusion and occlusion, extends beyond the frame; the film attributes theatricality to the referenced world."[42] Even when characters (like Christine and Saint-Aubin) seem to step off the stage, they remain on a more fundamental one. They continue to perform the rules of the game precisely when they seem to step outside the domain of these rules.

When André finally discovers Saint-Aubin and Christine together, the performance turns into a brawl but nonetheless remains a performance. The fight lacks any appearance of spontaneity and has none of the violence that one would expect in a genuine brawl. André fights because he believes that this is what one does in such a situation, just as Saint-Aubin proposes a duel out of a different, though related, belief. In both cases, the unwritten rules dictate their actions, and this gives a tangible stiffness to the fight, even though André claims to be overcome by emotion.

The intractability of performance and disguise becomes clearest in one of the most comic sections in the film during the lengthy period of time when Octave attempts to remove his bear costume. The other characters chose less elaborate costumes and thus have an easier job unmasking themselves. But Octave's inability to take off his costume functions as a synecdoche for the role that the costume plays within the world of *The Rules of the Game*. No one can free herself or himself from the costume. The characters not only wear masks or costumes for the masquerade; their entire identity is wrapped up in a performance, and they evince no substance beneath this performance.

We see this absence of substance in the second act that the film shows—the *danse macabre* or dance of death. As with the initial act, Renoir begins with a shot of the piano, but this time he shows the piano playing on its own. Here, there is no clear difference between the real pianist and the automatic player piano, but the absence of a piano player foreshadows a performance of absences—ghosts and skeletons. This act highlights the disappearance of the subject into the performance of the symbolic role, which is a form of death. The machine functions on its own without a living player, just as the symbolic role functions on its own without an individual agent.

The masquerade provides a comic respite from the violence of the hunt. But Renoir films the two scenes so that they bleed into each other. The hunt is a masquerade, and the masquerade is a hunt. Characters perform hunting, and both André and Schumacher hunt Saint-Aubin and Marceau during the masquerade. This overlapping of the two scenes illustrates how masks facilitate violence, despite the immediacy that we associate with violent acts.

## The absence of a ghost in the machine

The role that the machine plays in the film operates in parallel to the role of the mask. This is why Renoir gives a machine a part in the masquerade. At the climax of the performance, Robert takes the stage and introduces the star of the proceeding. This star is not a character in disguise but the immense music box that includes several automated figures on its exterior. These figures replicate Robert's many small mechanical figures that play music or perform some other action. Renoir focuses our attention on Robert's fascination with these machines and with the music box to expose the imaginary status of all vitality. The machines imitate life, but this imitation is the only life in the filmic universe. The automatons evince as much vitality as the people in *The Rules of the Game* in order to show that vitality is itself is a production rather than a naturally occurring phenomenon.

Given the role of the machine in *The Rules of the Game*, it is tempting to interpret Renoir as a humanist director formulating a critique of the control that we have ceded to the machine in modernity. This is one of the common interpretations of Renoir as a filmmaker, and it seems to follow from the nature of the depiction of the machine in the film. One can understand why Penelope Gilliatt would label *The Rules of the Game* "a great work of humanism."[43] Though Renoir expresses humanistic sentiments when he discusses the film, this type of interpretation cannot do justice to the constitutive role that mechanism plays in the film.

The problem with the position that views Renoir as a humanist critic of technological development is that the human beings in the film are themselves imitating life when they act. In this sense, they are no different than Robert's *oiseaux méchaniques* or mechanical birds. In each case, the vitality on display is a performance rather than an organic process. This is why it is wholly appropriate that the music box is the star performer in the masquerade. The mechanical bird is not a betrayal of spontaneous natural life but the model for it. In the filmic world that Renoir creates, the machine has an absolute priority relative to the natural world, and this priority is precisely what the subject must confront. Humanism attempts to retreat from it. But this is not the only misreading of the film that its depiction of machines generates.

Critics who see the film as a contrast between the traditional values of Robert and the new values of André also notice a contrast between the types of machine that each deals with. According to this position, Robert's mechanical birds are products of the nineteenth century, while André's plane and car are twentieth-century inventions. But this emphasis on the difference between Robert and André's machines overlooks the similar role that they have in the film. Robert's machines perform vitality and play a central part in his own performance. The same holds for André's machines.

Due to his association with technology, André seems like an emblem of modernity in contrast with Robert, the figure of tradition.[44] The film begins with the ado that accompanies André's transatlantic flight, and another important event in the film also centers on André using a machine. Not long after his arrival in Paris, we see André driving with Octave. Depressed by the absence of Christine at his arrival in Paris, André drives his car into a ditch. These two events mark the only interjections of modern technological machines in the film, and they represent a contrast with Robert's mechanical birds and Schumacher's guns, which are not linked to modernity and the twentieth century in the way that the plane and the car are.

But despite this difference, André's more advanced machines function in the film just like Robert's and Schumacher's.[45] For each of these characters, the machine provides a platform for performance. The machine itself performs and extends the performance of the character. André uses the plane to display his heroism to Christine rather than out of an intrinsic devotion to the act itself, and he uses the car to perform a suicidal gesture without actually committing suicide. Renoir shoots the crash in a way that emphasizes the performativity involved in it. We see a long shot of the car suddenly careen into the ditch without an interior shot of André's act of turning the car, an absence that renders the act completely artificial. Furthermore, it is significant that André's transatlantic flight occurs a decade after Charles Lindbergh's initial one. André copies Lindbergh rather than acting originally, even with his apparently great accomplishment. André's use of the machine as a vehicle for performance mirrors that of Robert rather than contrasting with it. But there is a different manifestation of technology in another of Renoir's films, and this difference highlights the role that the machine has in *The Rules of the Game*.

The machines in *The Rules of the Game* form a clear contrast with the machines in *La Bête humaine*. In the opening sequence of this earlier film, Renoir stresses the productive energy of the train, and he associates this productivity with the engineer who runs the train. Here, the machine does not imitate vitality but genuinely evinces it, just like the engineer Jacques Lantier (Jean Gabin). As a result of this genuine vitality, both the train and Jacques are dangerous forces in the world. The train moves with such speed and power that it threatens to destroy whatever lies in its path, and Jacques becomes pathologically violent whenever he drinks.

*La Bête humaine* is not a celebration of the machine. The film exposes the dangers of the train and the toll that the machine takes on the laborer. But it also extols the virtue of production, a production that is entirely absent from *The Rules of the Game*. It is only in the later film that we see the absolute priority of reproduction over productivity. The machine produces only by reproducing, which means that even it functions through the mediation of the signifier.

*The Rules of the Game* and *La Bête humaine* depict the two sides of the machine—its imitativeness and its productivity. In the same way, they depict the two sides of the subject. The superiority of the later film lies in its ability to see the priority of the imitation. The subject in *The Rules of the Game* imitates the Other in order to adopt an acceptable symbolic identity. Whenever a character begins to deviate from this imitation, she or he quickly returns to the imitation, just like a machine that begins working properly again after a brief breakdown.

## The exception becomes the rule

Most films that adopt a critical position relative to the world they depict include an exception within this world not subjected to critique. The exception exists to provide spectators a point of reference with which they can locate themselves, a manifestation of resistance to the world criticized. This is the case even in the bleakest and most critical films. Lars von Trier's *Melancholia* (2011) provides a nearly unremitting critique of our society's disavowal of trauma, and yet he shows one character, Justine (Kirsten Dunst), who is able to confront trauma and thus face the destruction of the world in a way that no one else can. Her presence in the film testifies to the possibility of an exception that escapes the critique.

Even if a film doesn't include an exceptional character like Justine in *Melancholia*, it structurally poses the camera as an exception to the world it depicts. The film distances itself from what it shows through the act of showing it. Darren Aronofsky's *Requiem for a Dream* (2000) has no exceptional characters: everyone succumbs to the destructiveness of the fantasy of the ultimate enjoyment and becomes completely debased as a result. But the critical attitude that the film takes up toward the characters evinces distance from them and places the film's position of enunciation as the exception. The spectator can watch *Requiem for a Dream* with the distance that the film takes up and thereby remain removed from its otherwise all-encompassing critique. For structural reasons, no film can eliminate the exceptional position altogether, which necessarily leaves the spectator an escape hatch. But a film can make clear how the exception is implicated in the diegetic world even in its exceptional position. This is what Renoir accomplishes in *The Rules of the Game* and why its achievement outstrips that of Lars von Trier in *Melancholia* and Aronofsky in *Requiem for a Dream*.

Though André initially appears as an exception, his status as a full-fledged part of the social structure becomes evident not long into the film. Likewise, Christine's exceptional status—she is an Austrian living in France—soon proves to be merely illusory. Renoir poses both of them as exceptions and then undercuts this position. With Octave, the film places him in the position of the exception throughout most of its running time. It is only at the conclusion that he falls back into the crowd. Renoir chooses himself to play the part of Octave and then grants Octave an exceptional status in order to reflect the exceptional position of the film itself in relation to the world it shows. When Octave loses his exceptional position, Renoir deprives the spectator of the last refuge from the rule of the social order and implicates the film itself in its critique.

Every exception in *The Rules of the Game* becomes part of the rule, and this trajectory reveals to spectators their investment in the world being criticized. One cannot watch *The Rules of the Game* from a safe distance because Renoir doesn't film it from a safe distance. The point is not simply that Renoir places himself in a certain position in the film but that he initially posits an exception that suddenly loses its exceptionality. By portraying himself in the role of the exception becoming the rule, Renoir metaphorically indicates what occurs with the film itself. Like every film, *The Rules of the Game* distances the spectator from the world that it depicts, but it subsequently collapses the distance and thrusts the spectator into this world.

Even on the surface, Octave is an unexceptional exception. He is not the main character of the film but part of an ensemble cast in which André and Christine seem to be the central figures. Octave is an exception not just because the director of the film plays him but because he sees through the rules that the others blindly follow. He quickly discerns that André heeds more the rules of heroic propriety than his desire for Christine, and later he stands out by not joining in the hunting party that includes the other would-be exceptions André and Christine (who even expresses her indifference toward hunting). Finally, the film shows Octave becoming overtaken with his love for Christine, so much so that he decides to leave with her. Here, his status as exception to the rule that subsumes the other characters is clear.

Octave walks with Christine outside the château after the melee with Schumacher and Marceau, and he recounts the failure of his life to her. He proposes heading back to the château, but Christine doesn't want to return. Instead, they enter a greenhouse, which functions as an exceptional space in the film. This is the only time that we see the greenhouse, and it is an isolated space of vitality that contrasts with the strict obedience to rules that governs the rest of the estate.

It is not coincidental that after the murder of André, which occurs outside the greenhouse, Robert inexplicably tells Schumacher to make the greenhouse off-limits. This gesture makes no sense unless we understand the greenhouse's status as an exceptional space, a space where one can genuinely violate the rules of the game. The greenhouse is not a crime scene, and yet Robert treats it as one because it is the site where a real transgression took place. In the exceptional space of the greenhouse, Christine can declare her love for Octave, and he can recognize that he loves her as well. But one cannot remain in the greenhouse. Octave proposes that they take the train and leave together. Before leaving, he returns to the château to retrieve Christine's coat, an action that ends up ruining their plans. The problem is that Octave cannot sustain his exceptionality no matter how much we might want him to. But the moment at which he capitulates is revelatory. The moment at which the exception ceases to be the exception creates an encounter with the gaze for the spectator.

The gaze in a film is the point at which the spectator's distance from the screen evaporates. In the encounter with the gaze, the spectator recognizes that her or his desire shapes what transpires on the screen, that the events occur through this desire rather than outside of it. This happens in *The Rules of the Game* when the exception proves to be part of the rule. Even though the hunting scene is the most celebrated scene in the film, the scene in which Octave gives up the possibility of leaving with Christine is the decisive scene. It is the enactment of an encounter with the gaze for the spectator. Renoir reveals the gaze in the film's most finely structured shot, when Lisette tells Octave that he cannot have a successful love relation with Christine.

After leaving Christine in the greenhouse with the promise to return with her coat, Octave enters the château. At the beginning of the scene, Renoir contrasts Octave with André and

Robert. We see André and Robert discussing their appreciation for friendship as Robert prepares to hand his spouse off to André, and Lisette is visible in the background far behind them. Octave enters even further in the distance behind her, and he enters just as André and Robert walk out of the scene in the foreground. Whereas deep focus in *The Rules of the Game* typically indicates the identity of the different levels in the shot, here the coincidence of the departure of the characters from the foreground and Octave's entrance in the background creates a contrast between them.[46] It is as if Octave at this point in the film cannot exist in the same shot with characters enmeshed in the rules like André and Robert. His entrance is the entrance of exceptionality and a refusal of the rules, and it drives them out of the shot.

Once inside the château, Octave sends Lisette for Christine's coat while he grabs his own and subsequently looks for his hat. When Lisette returns, she chastises Octave for his plan to run away with Christine, arguing first that he is too old for her and then that he lacks the wealth to keep her happy. Neither of these arguments convince Octave, but then Lisette adds, "Madame ne sera pas heureuse avec vous" ("Madame will not be happy with you"). This statement proves decisive. It leads him to abandon his desire to begin a relationship with Christine and to give her coat to André so that he can leave with her. This dramatic turn of events takes place within a matter of seconds while Lisette and Octave are talking in front of a mirror.

As Lisette begins to make her case, she and Octave are visible in the middle of the image, and the mirror is behind them on the right. Octave walks away in search of his hat, but he remains visible through the mirror after he retrieves it. When he returns to a position in front of the mirror, Lisette makes the argument about Christine's future unhappiness that ultimately convinces him. Due to the positioning of Octave and Lisette in relation to the camera and the mirror, we cannot see Octave's face at the precise moment he decides to abandon Christine. Prior to this instant of the decision, Octave's face is not visible directly but appears in the mirror. But just after Lisette says that Christine will not be happy with him, the back of her head obscures the spectator's view of his face in the mirror, so that the instant of the decision is absent within the visual field. Not only does Octave's face disappear from view when he gives up Christine but it disappears behind Lisette's head, indicating that Octave has become at this moment just like the others. He opts for the rules of the game.

Most often, the gaze is exceptional. It is a point that stands out in a film, like the shot in which the car temporarily stops sinking into the swamp in *Psycho* (Alfred Hitchcock 1960) or the appearance of the naked and beaten Dorothy Vallens (Isabella Rossellini) on the front lawn in *Blue Velvet* (David Lynch 1986). But in *The Rules of the Game*, the gaze emerges through the elimination of the exception, at the point when it becomes clear that no one escapes playing by the rules, even those who seem to have done so successfully. Here, the gaze disrupts the spectator's safe distance from the events on the screen by revealing the insidious power of the rules. They deprive the exception of its exceptionality, and this holds for the spectator as well. The position outside is implicated in the diegetic world inside the film, and the implication becomes apparent in the gaze. The spectator's inability to see Octave's face at the crucial instant attests to a blind spot in the field of vision, but it is this blind spot that attracts the subject's desire and makes manifest the subject's desire.

The blind spot in the field of vision marks the subject's absence of mastery over this field. More than any other sense, vision connotes mastery over the seen. But at the same time, the visual field appears to exist independently of our act of seeing. When we see events take place, we believe that they occur without reference to the desire of the subject seeing them. The gaze indicates, however, that the visual field exists for the sake of the onlooker, that this field is constructed around the desire of the subject looking. In the case of *The Rules of the Game*, the absence of Octave's face as he decides not to leave with Christine shows that the spectator can't see the most important element in the visual field and that this field has been constructed as a lure for the spectator's desire. We are implicated in the visual field through what we can't see.

It is significant that Octave's face doesn't simply disappear but becomes obscured by the head of a servant. As is clear throughout, the servants in the film are not proletarians on the edge of revolt but equal partners in the rules of the game with their masters. In this case, Lisette disciplines Octave and brings him back into the domain of the unwritten rules. After this encounter with Lisette that renders Octave's face an absence in the visual field, he completely abandons his plan to leave with Christine and returns to the symbolic identity that both Robert and André impute to him when they agree one can have "confiance" (trust) in him. This trust stems from Octave's symbolic position, which he temporarily rejects after proclaiming his love for Christine.

In the aftermath of Lisette's reproval, Octave hands Christine's coat to André and gives him his own coat, an action that quickly leads to André's death. But the significance of this action lies in Octave's abandonment of his enjoyment for that of André. It is not that Octave is self-sacrificing and fits the description that Robert and André give of him but that he accepts that he cannot be an exception to the rules of the game. Love without any wealth would place him outside of these rules, and Octave cedes Christine to André rather than leave the safety of the rules.

The scene involving Lisette and Octave is the crucial scene in the film. But it does not appear in the 81-minute version of the film that Renoir created after its initial rejection by the French public. Renoir admits that he took out scenes that he felt were likely to offend audiences, and this one certainly qualifies. It doesn't exculpate Octave but extends his culpability to the servant Lisette and to the spectator in the form of an encounter with the gaze. This encounter marks the traumatic highlight of the film, and it only exists in the film thanks to the reconstruction performed by Jean Gaborit and Jacques Maréchal. One can imagine enjoying *The Rules of the*

*Game* without this scene, but it provides a key for unlocking the nature of one's enjoyment.

The fact that Renoir removed this scene at some point during the film's tortured release—it is unclear if its removal occurred before or after the premiere—attests to the disruptiveness of the gaze. Renoir believed that removing this scene would make the film more palatable for audiences, but the gaze always has a double edge to it. On the one hand, it marks a moment of trauma for the spectator; on the other hand, it orients the spectator's enjoyment of the film. When we see the disappearance of Octave's face as he makes a decision (which is not at all *his* decision), we see our own disappearance as well. But this disappearance is also the point at which we enter into the film.

## An absence of romance

The end of *The Rules of the Game* cannot but strike the spectator as disappointing. The film focuses on the question of whom Christine will choose as it depicts her moving from one lover to another. It creates the expectation that it will conclude with her deciding to leave with André or Octave or Saint-Aubin. A romantic union promises to break the monotony of the ceaseless obedience on display throughout the film. But the last-minute capitulation of Octave and the gunshot from Schumacher eliminate the possibility of a romantic union and doom Christine to her unsatisfying existence with Robert. There can be no satisfying romantic union because the characters remain within the rules of the game. A satisfying romance exists, the film implies, only outside the domain of these rules.

The most common ideological fantasy that Hollywood films proffer is the romantic union. A film concludes with a couple uniting after undergoing a crisis or a series of struggles. The romantic union has an ideological function because it indicates that it is possible to overcome an intractable antagonism and achieve a harmonious relation. This fantasy is a staple of romantic comedies, but it populates dramas and action films as well. The romantic union occurs at the end of *When Harry Met Sally* (Rob Reiner 1989)—and at the end of films as disparate as *An Officer and a Gentleman* (Taylor Hackford 1982) and *The Bourne Identity* (Doug Liman 2002). In these cases and innumerable others, the romantic union at the conclusion of the film indicates an immersion in the ideological fantasy and a retreat from the exploration of antagonism.

Renoir doesn't just refuse this ideological fantasy in *The Rules of the Game*. He also emphasizes why it is impossible. The film hints at the possibility of a romantic union—first with Octave and Christine and then with André and Christine. But the servants (Lisette and Schumacher) prevent its accomplishment. Lisette deters Octave from returning to Christine, and Schumacher kills André when he goes to her. Renoir doesn't include these actions by the servants in order to indict them for the romantic failures of the masters but in order to indicate how the very existence of servants—the strictures of class society—function as a barrier to desire.

More importantly, Renoir evacuates the potential romantic union of all its significance. We see that André cares more for the rules of heroism and propriety than he does for Christine. Even if Schumacher didn't shoot him as he went to Christine, they would not have constituted a romantic union. Both Christine and André are incapable of participating in a romance because they are too preoccupied with participating in the societal game.

In order to enter into a romantic union, one would have to value the other's desire above one's own symbolic identity and the rules of the game that undergird that identity. The subject in a romance replaces the big Other with the little other, the social rules with the romantic partner. In doing so, this subject embraces the disruptiveness that accompanies the other's desire, and this is the step that no one in the film can take.

Most films use romance to assert their capitulation to the demands of ideology. Renoir avoids it in order to expose the prevalence of this capitulation. He creates a world in which romance is not even possible. This impossibility causes the conclusion of the film to stand out against the background of thousands of successful romantic unions on screen. It is not enough, of course, to show the failure of a particular romantic union. But Renoir takes the next step and clarifies why the romance is not even possible. Christine remains with Robert even at the moments when she's leaving him. There is no romance under the thrall of the obedience evinced in the world of *The Rules of the Game*.

## Renoir's gaze

One can identify specific moments where we encounter the gaze in Renoir's cinema, like the scene where Lisette obscures Octave's face in the mirror as he accepts her judgment and gives up the dream of leaving with Christine. Such moments stand out and testify to the precision with which Renoir can form a scene in order to resonate with the spectator and force the spectator to encounter her or his own desire in this moment. But his great accomplishment lies in the creation of a film style that constantly confronts the spectator with her or his desire made manifest within the visual field. He does this through a filmmaking style that predominates not only in *The Rules of the Game* but also throughout his cinema.

Renoir's characteristic shot involves a moving camera that discovers an obstruction or barrier in the field of vision. The combination of the moving camera and the obstruction provides a perfect vehicle for indicating the gaze. The movement of the camera has the effect of subjectivizing it and imbuing it with desire. Renoir's camera doesn't pretend to be a neutral observer of a neutral visual field but moves around in order to see the events that compel its vision.

The movement of the camera alone would not reveal desire's disturbance of the visual field. An omnipotent and neutral look could move around just as easily as a desiring one. But Renoir adds a series of disruptions to this look that confound its pretension to omnipotence and expose it as desiring. The obstacles that the moving camera encounters spur it on to look further and constitute the camera's look as a desiring look. This interaction of the moving camera with the obstacles that it encounters provides a constant enactment of the gaze in Renoir's cinema. This operation strips the camera and the spectator of their illusion of neutrality. The shot involving a moving camera that encounters an obstacle is the definitive Renoir shot, and though he doesn't have a monopoly on it, his extensive use of it marks his most important contribution to the formation of a cinema that addresses the gaze.

An exemplary scene occurs near the end of *The Rules of the Game* as Schumacher chases Marceau through the château with his gun. One particular shot begins with a pan that shows a group of people dancing to the music of Robert's music box. When Marceau enters followed by Schumacher, the film tracks the chase, but it doesn't keep the two of them constantly visible. Both temporarily disappear behind people dancing, so that an obstacle to the spectator's look appears. These obstacles that populate Renoir's cinema are manifestations of the gaze when they disrupt the seemingly omnipotent look of the moving camera.

Renoir's achievement does not reside only in one type of shot but in an approach to the cinema that this type of shot exemplifies. He constantly implicates the spectator in what she or he sees. The spectator's desire is at the heart of the visual field in Renoir's films. He lays a trap for the gaze and foregrounds our experience as desiring subjects.

For historians of film, Renoir's importance centers not so much on his own work as on the filmmakers that he influences. He has a legitimate claim to being the parent figure for both Italian Neorealism and for the French New Wave. Both movements learned from him as a filmmaker and found formal inspiration in his films. His preference for deep focus, location shooting, and filmic shots paves the way for these important movements in the history of cinema. Though everyone acknowledges the importance of Renoir's own films, there is a tendency to think of him as a precursor. But his own films reward our close attention. *The Rules of the Game*, more than any other of his films, rewards our attention by making clear our failures. One looks at this film and discovers the trauma of one's own capitulation and unconscious investment in that capitulation. But at the same time, the film confronts the spectator with the equally traumatic possibility of escaping that capitulation and discovering the subject of freedom. When we see how we capitulate, we see the possibility for not doing so.

# Notes

1   Just to be clear, in contrast to a critic like André Bazin, I do not count *The River* as one of his great achievements.

2   *Boudu Saved from Drowning* anticipates the critique that Renoir develops in *The Rules of the Game*, but it lacks the formal achievement of involving the spectator in the object of the critique. One can watch *Boudu Saved from Drowning* without experiencing oneself as the target of the critique along with the polite bourgeois society depicted in the film.

3   William Rothman, *The "I" of the Camera: Essays in Film Criticism, History, and Aesthetics*, 2nd ed. (Cambridge: Cambridge University Press, 2003), 129–30.

4   In *Citizen Kane*, Welles's focus is not on unconscious investment in obedience but on the unconscious sources of capitalist accumulation, which makes the film a threat not just to Hearst but to the American social order as such.

5   There are a variety of theories that attempt to account for the frosty reception that the film received. Perhaps the film's foremost admirer André Bazin argues that it is the sheer

complexity of *The Rules of the Game* that the public could not accept. In his posthumous book on Renoir, he argues that "it is a work that reveals itself only gradually to the spectator, even if he is attentive" (André Bazin, *Jean Renoir*, trans. W. W. Halsey II and William H. Simon [New York: Simon and Schuster, 1973], 83). My argument is the opposite: the public rejected *The Rules of the Game* not because it is too unclear but because it is too clear in its critique.

6   One could historicize the critique that the film makes—and Renoir himself does this when speaking about the film—but doing so misses the nature of the critique. The psychic investment in obedience is not confined to France in the late 1930s and early 1940s but proliferates in every social formation. Historicizing the film represents an attempt to limit its critical scope and exempt oneself from this critique.

7   This is the controlling idea in Kafka's universe, and we see the seductive effect of the inconsistent law in the actions of Joseph K. in *The Trial*.

8   Critic Alan Vanneman argues that the film isn't really critical in the last instance of the society that it depicts. Vanneman states, "For all his criticism of the hollowness of aristocratic society, Renoir can't imagine—wouldn't want to imagine—anything to replace it. To live for style, for perfect manners—to live in the grand manner—surely that is everything!" Alan Vanneman, "Who Do You Love?: Jean Renoir's *Rules of the Game* Reconsidered," *Bright Lights Film Journal* 60 (2008): http://www.brightlightsfilm.com/60/60rules.php#.U3tVYhyMTw4.

9   We cannot know the precise running time of the initial version of the film or the premiere version because neither version still exists. There has thus been considerable critical dispute about these figures.

10   There are critics who argue that Renoir overstates the negativity that greeted the film on its release, but they have the status of contemporary scientists who doubt whether human activity contributes to global warming. Claude Gauteur is the most outspoken of these debunkers of the legend, but while Gauteur is able to produce positive reviews of the film at the time of its release and to note the

absence of any excessive censorship (relative to Renoir's other films), he makes no attempt to explain why Renoir had to engage in repeated actions of self-censorship. But even Gauteur reluctantly admits that "among the favorable critiques, few were without reservation ... while practically all the negative critiques were unqualified. In addition, the so-called important press, that which at the time had the largest audience, was violently *against*, those *for*, with or without reservation, had in contrast a lesser print run and circulation" (Claude Gauteur, *D'un Renoir l'autre* [Paris: Le Temps des Cérises, 2005], 137). Gauteur goes on to suggest that hostility was the effect of Renoir's self-censorship rather than its cause, that Renoir's cuts rendered a fully acceptable film unintelligible to the audiences of the time. While it is undoubtedly the case that some film historians have exaggerated the negative reception of the film, to blame Renoir's cuts for it fails to consider that the appreciation for the film emerged in response to an even more truncated version. If Renoir's modifications made the film unintelligible for initial critics and audiences, it would have remained so for André Bazin and François Truffaut.

11 V. F. Perkins, *La Règle du jeu* (London: BFI, 2012), 8–9.

12 Though the original 94-minute version no longer exists, a copy of the edited 81-minute film does.

13 Perkins, *La Règle du jeu*, 10–11.

14 In a video essay produced for the Criterion DVD of *The Rules of the Game*, Renoir scholar Chris Faulkner contends that reconstruction adds scenes that blunt the critical edge of the film, which is much more evident even in the highly edited 81-minute version. According to Faulkner, the explanatory details that come out in the reconstruction have the effect of mitigating the critique of several characters, especially Octave, who appears much more complicit in André's death in the 81-minute version. Though this judgment is appealing and seems correct when looking at the two versions side by side (as Faulkner does), it doesn't grasp how the increased details about the characters have the effect of enhancing the spectator's sense of their capitulation to the rules of the game. The more attractive the characters become, the more their capitulation stands out.

15 James Leahy, "Jean Renoir," *Senses of Cinema* (March 2003): http://sensesofcinema.com/2003/great-directors/renoir/.

16 Renoir's rejection of national antagonism in *La Grande Illusion* is also part of his antifascism. The fascist depends on a strong nation-state that opposes itself to other nation-states, and this vision has no place in Renoir's film.

17 Maréchal's defiant singing of "La Marseillaise" not only expresses his defiance of his German captors but identifies him with revolutionary France. In *Casablanca* (1942), Michael Curtiz alludes to Maréchal's defiance when he has Victor Laszlo (Paul Henreid) lead the band at Rick's in an impromptu rendition of "La Marseillaise" in order to rally the occupied French living under Vichy rule in Morocco.

18 The role that class antagonism plays in *La Grande Illusion* precludes any interpretation that focuses on the humanity that all the characters in the film share. This is the misstep that Irving Singer makes in his analysis of the film. While Singer correctly sees the unimportance of national identity in the film, he doesn't pay enough attention to the role of class antagonism. If the film highlights class antagonism, it cannot simultaneously bespeak Renoir's humanism. Antagonism is antithetical to the idea of a shared human substance since the idea of antagonism is that every substance suffers from an internal division that leads to external ones. But according to Singer's humanistic reading, "We are not encouraged to see the Germans as a breed apart. The problem is how to make contact with them and establish a sense of mutual humanity." Irving Singer, *Three Philosophical Filmmakers: Hitchcock*, *Welles*, *Renoir* (Cambridge, MA: MIT Press, 2004), 185.

19 In Robert Altman's loose remake of *The Rules of the Game* entitled *Gosford Park* (2001), the antagonism between the nobility and their servants is the film's fundamental preoccupation. Class division actually leads to the murder around which the mystery of the film is structured. In this sense, despite the clear allusions to *The Rules of the Game* (like the repetition of the hunting scene), *Gosford Park* actually has more in common with *La Grande Illusion* than with Renoir's later film.

20 It is significant that the upper class depicted in *The Rules of the Game* is not uniformly aristocratic, as it is in *La Grande*

*Illusion*. Though Robert is a marquis and others at the party have aristocratic titles, the film primarily shows the haute bourgeoisie rather than the aristocracy.

21  The lack of allegiance with the lower class earns *The Rules of the Game* the opprobrium of some critics, including Martin O'Shaughnessy in his book *Jean Renoir*. O'Shaughnessy upbraids Renoir for the negative portrayal of the lower class, which represents a contrast with his earlier films. Though he takes issue with O'Shaughnessy's negative judgment on the film, Ian Johnston accepts the contention that *The Rules of the Game* represents an abandonment of earlier political commitments. He writes,

> *La Règle du jeu* is the peak and summation of all the work Renoir had done in France in the thirties, but it also represents a substantial break with that work and a break, too, with the left-wing, Popular Front principles found in the earlier films. Gone are the class-based concerns for social justice, the favoring of the working class over the upper classes, the portrayal of totally negative exploiters of the working class like Batala (*Le Crime de Monsieur Lange*, 1935) or Kostilev (*Les Bas-Fonds*, 1936) who are judged as deserving to die for their economic crimes. Instead, upper and lower classes are viewed as two sides of the same coin, with characters from each class paralleling and reflecting each other, and with all classes conniving at hiding the truth of the tragedy at the film's dénouement, pasting over the cracks revealed in the surface of French society so that the game can continue: this is the ultimate "rule of the game." (Ian Johnston, *La Règle du jeu*, *The Film Journal* 11: http://www.thefilmjournal.com/issue11/rulesofthegame.html/)

While Johnston is correct to see that the film reveals the parallel between the upper and lower classes, he fails to note that this represents an extension of the leftist politics of Renoir's earlier films. Highlighting the complicity of the lower class is propaedeutic to emancipation from this complicity, not an endorsement of it.

22  Ironically, criminals are often the most vigilant members of a society in upholding its unwritten rules, even as they openly flout its written laws. This finds a traditional expression in the idea of "honor among thieves."

23  Jacques Lacan, *The Seminar of Jacques Lacan, Book VII: The Ethics of Psychoanalysis, 1959-1960*, ed. Jacques-Alain Miller, trans. Dennis Porter (New York: Norton, 1992), 315.

24  The translation of Robert's dialogue (and all the dialogue cited from the film) is my own and doesn't correspond exactly to the subtitles on the Criterion DVD.

25  Stanley Cavell, *The World Viewed: Reflections on the Ontology of Film*, enlarged ed. (Cambridge, MA: Harvard University Press, 1979), 222.

26  Cavell interprets the final scene as the victory of cinema over the theater as much as that of Schumacher and his gun over Robert and his sense of propriety.

27  See Sigmund Freud, *The Psychopathology of Everyday Life*, in *The Standard Edition of the Complete Psychological Works of Sigmund Freud*, vol. 6, ed. and trans. James Strachey, (London: Hogarth Press, 1960), 1–279.

28  As if to prove the thesis that artists are often the worst interpreters of their own work, in his autobiography, Renoir claims that André is truly an outsider who fails to follow the rules of the game. He insists on "the purity of Jurieu, the victim, who, trying to fit into a world to which he does not belong, fails to respect the rules of the game." Jean Renoir, *My Life and My Films*, trans. Norman Denny (New York: Atheneum, 1974), 170.

29  As Raymond Durgnat puts it, "In *La Règle du jeu* no one and everyone is to blame" (Raymond Durgnat, *Jean Renoir* [Berkeley: University of California Press, 1974], 200). Whether knowingly or not, Durgnat here uses the same terms that Martin Heidegger uses to describe what he calls *das Man* ("the they"), the force of anonymous social authority that Jacques Lacan would later call the big Other. Heidegger insists that "the they" is everyone and no one. The central character in *The Rules of the Game* is "the they," which exists through a collective enacting of it.

30  While accepting that the film explores the power of unwritten rules, Colin Davis contends that Robert's concluding statement that transforms Schumacher's act of murder into an accident represents a case of a character changing the rules while

appearing to follow them. According to this interpretation of the film's conclusion, Renoir ends the film on an optimistic note. As Davis states, "With the Marquis as its self-appointed helmsman, this society is not as stagnant, nor as *inevitably* doomed as the film's sociological critics have tended to argue. He is the Wittgensteinian bluffer who can change the rules by pretending he was following them all along." Colin Davis, *Scenes of Love and Murder: Renoir, Film and Philosophy* (London: Wallflower, 2009), 114.

31   Though Renoir uses depth of field in his earlier films, it becomes much more common in *The Rules of the Game*. He shoots almost every scene in deep focus, which forces the spectator to emphasize it when interpreting the film.

32   The theoretical opposition between André Bazin (the champion of deep focus) and Sergei Eisenstein (the champion of montage) is also a political opposition. It is not the difference between right and left but between two visions of political emancipation. Bazin's vision involves the filmmaker ceding authority to the spectator, while Eisenstein's relies on the filmmaker making the spectator's political situation clear to the spectator. The risk of the former is a failure to see where one stands politically, while the risk of the latter is the loss of a sense of oneself as an agent. This is why cinema cannot just choose between deep focus and montage but must utilize both, as Renoir himself does to great effect in the famous hunting scene from *The Rules of the Game*.

33   André Bazin, "The Evolution of the Language of Cinema," in *What Is Cinema?*, vol. 1, trans. Hugh Gray (Berkeley: University of California Press, 1967), 35–6.

34   Alexander Sesonske, *Jean Renoir: The French Films, 1924-1939* (Cambridge, MA: Harvard University Press, 1980), 433. The hunting scene has more cuts in it than occur in the entire rest of the film.

35   Renoir himself claims that he included the scene in the film as an explicitly political act designed to expose the barbarism of hunting.

36   Lacan posits that the subject is always divided between the subject of the enunciation (the subject who speaks) and the subject of the statement (the subject spoken about).

The unconscious exists through the failure of these two subjects to align with each other, and as a result, the subject always speaks from beyond where it locates itself. Lacan's attraction to Arthur Rimbaud's famous statement "Je est un autre" (I is an other) stems from its attempt to approximate the disjunction of the subject by distorting grammar.

37  In his interviews with François Truffaut, Hitchcock explains the difference between suspense and surprise in the following way:

We are now having a very innocent little chat. Let us suppose that there is a bomb underneath this table between us. Nothing happens, and then all of a sudden, "Boom!" There is an explosion. The public is *surprised*, but prior to this surprise, it has seen an absolutely ordinary scene, of no special consequence. Now, let us take a *suspense* situation. The bomb is underneath the table, and the public *knows* it, probably because they have seen the anarchist place it there. The public is *aware* that the bomb is going to explode at one o'clock and there is a clock in the decor. The public can see that it is a quarter to one. In these conditions the same innocuous conversation becomes fascinating because the public is participating in the scene. The audience is longing to warn the characters on the screen: "You shouldn't be talking about such trivial matters. There's a bomb beneath you and it's about to explode!"

In the first case we have given the public fifteen seconds of *surprise* at the moment of the explosion. In the second we have provided them with fifteen minutes of *suspense*. The conclusion is that whenever possible the public must be informed. Except when the surprise is a twist, that is, when the unexpected ending is, in itself, the highlight of the story. Alfred Hitchcock, qtd. in François Truffaut, *Hitchcock: The Definitive Study of Alfred Hitchcock by François Truffaut*, rev. ed. (New York: Simon and Schuster, 1985), 73.

38  Jean-Pierre Boon, "La Chasse, la règle et le mensonge: éléments structuraux dans *La Règle du jeu*," *The French Review* 53.3 (1980): 341.

39  The choice of taking up a symbolic identity is a forced choice because refusing it results in psychotic exclusion from the possibilities of the social order. Lacan compares the forced choice of symbolic identity to the thief's proclamation,

"Your money or your life!" One must give up one's money, or else one loses both money and life. Refusal deprives one of both elements at stake.

40   Christopher Faulkner, *The Social Cinema of Jean Renoir* (Princeton: Princeton University Press, 1986), 114. One might contrast the murder in *The Rules of the Game* not only with the individualizing murder in *The Crime of Monsieur Lange* but also with the collective murder that takes place in *The Lower Depths*. The difference between this murder and the murder of André is that the death of Kostylev (Vladimir Sokoloff) represents a collective and emancipatory action on the part of the lower class against an oppressive force. This act highlights class antagonism. The social order's murder of André is not a collective action and has the effect of smoothing over class antagonism.

41   Pierre Guislain, *La Règle du jeu—Jean Renoir* (Paris: Hatier, 1990), 95.

42   Karla Oeler, "Renoir and Murder," *Cinema Journal* 48.2 (2009): 37–8.

43   Penelope Gilliatt, *Jean Renoir: Essays, Conversations, Reviews* (New York: McGraw-Hill, 1975), 64.

44   Julia Lesage notes that the film refuses to elevate modernity as progress over tradition. She writes, "What Renoir refuses to do, and this is one of the virtues of the film, is to say that the modern (André) is better than the aristocrat (Robert) even though the film indicts aristocratic decadence." Julia Lesage, "*S/Z* and *Rules of the Game*," *Jump Cut* 12–13 (1976–77): http://www.ejumpcut.org/archive/.

45   As Christopher Faulkner points out, Robert's interest in machines is not confined to antiquaries, and this furthers the similarity with André. Faulkner writes, "Robert is shown to have a particular affinity for contemporary technology by way of his brand new 1938 right-hand drive Delahaye coach, his telephones, and his several radios, both in his Paris townhouse and at La Colinière, his country estate." Christopher Faulkner, "Musical Automata, *La Règle du jeu*, and the Cinema," *South Central Review* 28.3 (2011): 5.

46  The irony of this scene is that André and Robert praise Octave
    at the moment he is betraying their confidence by preparing
    to leave with Christine. But in the end, the film proves them
    correct because the unwritten rules seize Octave before he
    can act.

# Conclusion:
# Psychoanalytic film
# theory today

We watch films because in some way they arouse our desire. Trailers exist in order to entice us to spend our time with a film that promises to speak to us on the level of desire. The masterpieces of the cinema are the works that stimulate desire more than ordinary films, even if at first the only evidence for this desire was repression in the form of hostility or indifference. The films that don't arouse our desire at all are failures, and we most often simply stop watching or stop paying attention when a film falls into this category. The large majority of films fall in between these two categories, and we must examine them to see how they relate to our desire.

The question of desire and film is not a subjective question. Different spectators obviously have different desires. But desire is not external to the film. Though different spectators may respond in a variety of ways, each film's structure creates a specific deployment of desire and adopts a specific relationship to this desire. In this sense, we can speak about desire in cinema without falling into subjectivism or making allowances for differences among spectators. Clearly there will always be individuals who do not respond to the way a film structures desire. But spectatorship is internal to the film, and particular spectators can either adopt the position that the film produces or not. The task of interpretation doesn't refer to these particular variations. It lies instead in engaging the way desire is structured in the film. The empirical question of particular spectators does not change the structure of the film, which is where desire in the cinema lies.

The key role that desire plays in filmic spectatorship points to the importance of psychoanalysis for theorizing and analyzing film. Psychoanalysis emerges out of the disruption that desire causes in the social order, and it places this disruption at the center of its understanding of the subject and of society. As psychoanalysis discovers, the disruptiveness of desire both stimulates social productivity and threatens the stability of the social order. Subjects and societies must address desire's disruptiveness, and one way that they do so is through the production of films. Psychoanalysis enables us to investigate the effects of this disruptiveness and to become aware of how ideology attempts to contain it. The disruptiveness of desire is the source of all political acts and the ideological effort to forestall such acts.

Desire emerges through antagonism, and antagonism constantly poses a threat to the forces of social authority. Social authority employs ideology in order to hide the existence of antagonism and thus to convince subjects that their desire has a possible resolution. Without the existence of social antagonisms, we would be self-identical beings free of desire. The social order's inability to achieve a harmonious balance is the condition of possibility for the desiring subject. The direct relationship between antagonism and desire links desire to trauma. There is no desire free of trauma, which is why desire is often repressed. But film enables us to encounter the trauma of our desire and to enjoy this encounter. This is the source of the privilege that film has as both a site for radicalizing subjects and for disseminating ideology—for political contestation. Trauma in the cinema is not only traumatic; it is also enjoyable. The genius of film lies in its ability to subject us to a traumatic disruption that we can enjoy. Film is a primary political battleground today, and psychoanalytic theory shows how the battle is being waged and which forces are winning.

Film is a political battleground because films can arouse our desire in a way that exposes us to the trauma of antagonism or they can do so in a way that conceals the existence of antagonism. That is to say, the films that successfully arouse our desire don't do so in the same way or relate to desire in a uniform fashion. How a film relates to our desire provides a basis for how we can evaluate it. The great achievements in the history of cinema, like *The Rules of the Game*, demand that spectators encounter their own desire in what they see and hear in the form of the gaze and the voice. What's more, they refuse to offer spectators a path out of this encounter. Such films show that there is no solution to the trauma of desire and thus reveal that fantasy cannot deliver the subject or the social order from antagonism. This political achievement is accomplished only through the film's formal achievement and is unthinkable without it.

Films that utilize the gaze and voice to show the irreducibility of antagonism are not typical films, and they often receive the type of cool reception that *The Rules of the Game* did. Typical films present the trauma of desire as a soluble problem rather than an irreducible antagonism. They do so by providing the spectator a point of escape from this trauma, an ideological fantasy in which the spectator can envision the recovery of the impossible lost object and the satisfactory realization of desire. In this way, film can (and most often does) function ideologically, due undoubtedly in large part to the role that capital plays in film production. But there is no direct relationship between capitalist financing of a film and an ideological product. A film can always defy its conditions of production, and we can measure this defiance in psychoanalytic terms by insisting on the distinction that Jacques Lacan makes between the objet a and the object of desire.

The objet a triggers our desire, and yet at no time can we have this object. Whatever the quantity of objects that we obtain, the objet a persists as an absence that we can never have. The moment that the objet a appears on the verge of becoming present, we find that what appears is not this object that we anticipated and that oriented our desire. We relate to the objet a as a defining absence for our subjectivity. In light of the objet a, what is not present for us always counts infinitely more than what is. It is a singular object, precisely because it is never present among a series of empirical objects that are defined by their capacity to be exchanged with each other. The singularity of the objet a depends on its absence.

The object of desire, in contrast, is present, and thus it lacks any possible singularity. If a certain object of desire is missing, another will often suffice as a replacement. When a store runs out of the chocolate cupcakes that are the object of my desire, I can find some pleasure by substituting a piece of chocolate cake instead. I obtain my objects of desire all the time, and these objects are multiple. As long as I focus on the object of desire, satisfaction seems entirely within reach. I just have to work hard enough or have enough money and I can obtain the object of desire. The contrast with the objet a is radical, and the implications of thinking in terms of the object of desire instead of the objet a are laden with political consequences.

As long as I believe that I can obtain the object, I succumb to the fundamental ideological illusion. I become ready to invest myself in the inducements of the social order and to capitulate by whatever necessary measures in order to obtain the object. The lure of possibility creates a pliant subject for social authority, and cinema contributes to this pliancy by highlighting objects of desire at the expense of the impossible objet a.

This occurs most obviously in the action film where the hero eliminates a violent threat to the social order and in the romantic comedy where the couple overcomes the barriers that menace their relationship in order to form a sturdy romantic union. In both cases, antagonism produces desire in the spectator, but the films present a solution for desire and thus show the possibility of overcoming antagonism. While watching these types of films, the spectator obtains the object of desire and the objet a falls by the wayside in the midst of the fantasmatic resolution. Desire becomes a problem with a clear solution, and one leaves the cinema invested in the possibility of a solution.

Once I recognize that the impossible objet a orients my desire, I break from the ideological constraints that the social order produces. Though we might imagine that political subjectivity depends on an investment in obtaining the object of desire through the political act, Lacan argues that the true act has as its endpoint the objet a. As he says in his seminar on the psychoanalytic act, "The act (every act and not just the psychoanalytic act) promises to whomever takes it up only this end that I designate in the objet a."[1] One is capable of acting only when one doesn't expect to obtain something. The act enables one instead to sustain one's relationship to the absence of the objet a and even to identify oneself with this absence.

The encounter with the objet a is a freeing encounter for the subject. The absent status of this object enables the subject to understand that the social order has nothing substantial to offer it. The lures of ideology become evident as lures rather than as substantial objects that one might obtain and enjoy. The result of the turn from the object of desire to the objet a is freedom, but the cost of this freedom is a confrontation with trauma. One of the fundamental lessons of psychoanalysis is that there is no freedom without trauma because trauma occurs when we lose the social background that obscures our freedom.

Unlike the typical action film or romantic comedy that depicts the realization of desire, *The Rules of the Game* represents an opposed political possibility. It is a film that confronts the spectator with the irreducibility of antagonism by opting for the objet a instead of presenting the spectator with an obtainable object of desire. Renoir constantly foregrounds the spectator's involvement in the capitulation to the unwritten rules of society that he depicts in the characters. The famous hunting scene doesn't just criticize the cruelty of the hunt but makes the spectator's enjoyment dependent on this cruelty. And in the film's conclusion Renoir shows how Octave (Jean Renoir) capitulates to the rules of the game even at the moment when he seems to have escaped them. In this way, the film erects a series of obstacles to the realization of the spectator's desire, and it demonstrates that these obstacles are more important than the objects of desire that we might obtain. The spectator of the film cannot escape the trauma of her or his desire because the aesthetic that Renoir develops demands this encounter without providing a line of escape. The task of psychoanalytic film theory involves interpreting how films structure the spectator's experience of desire. This is where psychoanalysis can make a contribution that no other approach can provide.

Psychoanalysis is an investigation of the fecundity of the obstacle. Screen theory's failure to grasp this basic principle is the source of its failure as an incarnation of psychoanalysis in the study of cinema. What underlies Screen theory's approach to the cinema is a belief that the cinema frees us of obstacles. As Christian Metz puts it in *The Imaginary Signifier*,

> At the cinema, it is always the other who is on the screen; as for me, I am there to look at him. I take no part in the perceived, on the contrary, I am *all-perceiving*. All-perceiving as one says all-powerful (this is the famous gift of "ubiquity" the film gives its spectator); all-perceiving, too, because I am entirely on the side of the perceiving instance: absent from the screen, but certainly present in the auditorium, a great eye and ear without which the perceived would have no one to perceive it, the instance, in other words, which *constitutes* the cinema signifier (it is I who make the film).[2]

This conception of the spectator cannot explain why such a spectator would take an interest in that happens on the screen.

If the spectator is all-perceiving, she or he would have no desire to perceive. Film actually offers only a partial perception of the visual and aural fields. It engages us by throwing up obstacles, and we engage a film through what we don't see or hear, not what we do. It is only film's ability to present our desire with an obstacle in the form of the gaze or the voice that generates an interest in what's happening on the screen.

According to its many critics, psychoanalytic film theory misfired in its initial incarnation as Screen theory because it aimed too broadly and tried to produce a universal explanation of the cinema. But what characterizes Screen theory is, on the contrary, the narrowness of its preoccupations. Psychoanalysis has more to offer the understanding of cinema than analyses that criticize the cinematic apparatus or interpretations that focus on the mirror effect of the screen. It serves as an exploration for how the subject fantasizes, desires, and enjoys, and it does so through a focus on the obstacles to perception that the cinema establishes.

The point of psychoanalysis is that our desire is inimical to becoming all-perceiving. Ideological films can present the fantasy that we can overcome the obstacle to becoming all-perceiving, but in doing so, they deprive the subject of the opportunity to encounter itself as desiring. The obstacle that film places in the way of our perception is the source of its attractiveness, and this obstacle—the form of the objet a (the gaze or the voice)—is what causes us to watch a film and find it desirable. But the obstacle also provides an opportunity for the spectator to recognize herself or himself within the film and to see that the film is not just there to be seen. Every film is organized around the subject's desire and the subject's investment in what it sees. For psychoanalytic film theory, the real question is the attitude that a film takes up to the spectator's involvement. This standard enables us to see why *The Rules of the Game* is one of the most important achievements in the history of cinema. When we confront our desire on the screen, the revolutionary potential of film for the subject reaches its apex.

# Notes

1   Jacques Lacan, *Le Séminaire XV: L'Acte psychanalytique, 1967-1968*, unpublished manuscript, session of January 24, 1968.

2   Christian Metz, *The Imaginary Signifier: Psychoanalysis and Cinema*, trans. Celia Britton, Annwyl Williams, Ben Brewster, and Alfred Guzzetti (Bloomington: Indiana University Press, 1982), 48.

# FURTHER READING
## (FROM THE EASIEST TO
## THE MOST DIFFICULT)

Sigmund Freud, *Interpretation of Dreams*, trans. James Strachey (New York: Basic Books, 2010). This is the foundational work of psychoanalytic thought and Freud's most important for the analysis of film. Because of the close link between the logic of the dream and that of film, this work provides an ideal entry point into a more developed understanding of psychoanalytic film theory.

Sigmund Freud, *Beyond the Pleasure Principle*, trans. James Strachey (New York: Norton, 1961). Here, Freud discovers the death drive as a more fundamental structure in the psyche than the pleasure principle. In this sense, it represents a decisive break in the history of psychoanalysis and guides most recent psychoanalytic film theory. It is the pivotal work of the later Freud.

Bruce Fink, *The Lacanian Subject: Between Language and Jouissance* (Princeton: Princeton University Press, 1995). Fink's work clarifies the notorious difficulties of Lacan's theory and thus functions as a bridge from reading Freud to tackling Lacanian theory and the film theory influenced by Lacan.

Fabio Vighi, *Sexual Difference in European Cinema: The Curse of Enjoyment* (New York: Palgrave Macmillan, 2009). The book offers the most lucid explanation of how the central Lacanian concept of enjoyment (or jouissance) is deployed in the cinema. Vighi discusses several celebrated European films and directors in clear psychoanalytic terms.

Todd McGowan, *The Real Gaze: Film Theory After Lacan* (Albany: SUNY Press, 2007). This book takes the psychoanalytic concept of the gaze as its point of departure for developing a theory of the politics of cinematic spectatorship. The introductory chapter that sums up the theory of the gaze in cinema was published as a separate essay under the title "Lacanian Film Theory and Its Vicissitudes."

Slavoj Žižek, editor, *Everything You Always Wanted to Know about Lacan (But Were Afraid to Ask Hitchcock)* (London: Verso, 1992). Žižek's edited collection brings together many of the most important psychoanalytic theorists writing today, and Hitchcock serves as the perfect director for their exploration of a variety of psychoanalytic ideas.

Slavoj Žižek, *Looking Awry: An Introduction to Jacques Lacan through Popular Culture* (Cambridge: MIT Press, 1991). Though this work purports to be an introduction to Lacan through popular culture, one might equally see it as an introduction to film theory through Lacan. There are some literary examples, but most of Žižek's examples are from the cinema. He shows the interdependence of cinema and psychoanalytic theory through the discussion of many films.

Alenka Zupančič, *The Odd One In: On Comedy* (Cambridge: MIT Press, 2008). Zupančič's theory of comedy is not film specific, but she uses many filmic instances to explain it. In the process, she explores several key psychoanalytic concepts (such as the phallus, desire, and fantasy) as they appear in films.

Jacques Lacan, *Four Fundamental Concepts of Psychoanalysis*, trans. Alan Sheridan (New York: Norton, 1978). This is the seminar in which Lacan introduces the gaze and gives examples of how it manifests itself. Though he doesn't discuss the cinema, this seminar is his least difficult work, and its applicability to the cinema is readily apparent.

Joan Copjec—*Read My Desire: Lacan Against the Historicists* (Cambridge: MIT Press, 1994). Copjec's book provides the definitive critique of traditional psychoanalytic film theory by showing how this theory departs from the fundamental ideas of psychoanalysis for the sake of a historical approach to film. The key chapter, "The Orthopsychic Subject," was also published separately.

# INDEX

www.ingramcontent.com/pod-product-compliance
Ingram Content Group UK Ltd.
Pitfield, Milton Keynes, MK11 3LW, UK
UKHW031250020325
455689UK00008B/107